Beautiful Stories of Repenting Muslims

Muddassir Khan

Published by Muddassir Khan, 2024.

Table of Contents

Beautiful Stories

of

Repenting Muslims

Muddassir Khan

While every precaution has been taken in the preparation of this book, the publisher assumes no responsibility for errors or omissions, or for damages resulting from the use of the information contained herein.

Introduction

Indeed, all praise is due to Allah. We praise Him, seek His assistance, and ask for His forgiveness. We seek refuge in Allah from the evil of our own selves and from the bad deeds we have committed. Whomever Allah guides, there is no misleader for him, and whomever He leads astray, there is no guide for him. I bear witness that there is no deity except Allah, alone, without any partner, and I bear witness that Muhammad is His servant and Messenger.

To proceed:

Dear Readers!...... Peace be upon you and the mercy of Allah and His blessings.

The themes of the Noble Qur'an have been divided by scholars into three major sections:

1. Monotheism (Tawheed).

2. Legislation.

3. Stories, Narratives, and the History of Nations.

The impact of stories, narratives, and historical events cannot be denied. Considering their appeal to human nature, Allah has taken special care in His noble book, the Qur'an, to present various events, stories, and narratives of different nations and peoples from time to time, making the message more comprehensible.

In view of this the following stories are presented so that a person gains wisdom from these incidents and follows the straight path which leads to the pleasure of Allah and His paradise.

The Danger of Underestimating Sins

May Allah have mercy on you and me, you should know that Allah Almighty has commanded His servants to repent sincerely. Allah Almighty says: "O you who have believed, repent to Allah with sincere repentance." (Surah At-Tahrim)

And Allah has also granted us a period for repentance. One is the period before the noble scribes record the deed. The Prophet (peace be upon him) said: "The angel on the left raises the pen for six hours from the Muslim servant who commits a sin or makes a mistake. If he regrets and seeks forgiveness from Allah, it is not recorded, otherwise, it is written as one bad deed."

And the second period is from the time of writing until death. The calamity is that nowadays many people commit various kinds of sins day and night. There are some among them who consider sins to be trivial. You will see that many people regard minor sins as insignificant in their hearts. For example, one of them might say: "What harm is there in looking at a non-mahram woman or shaking hands with her?"

These people look at non-mahram women in magazines and serial articles secretly, until they know that it is forbidden, then some of them very easily ask, "How bad is it? Is it a major sin or a minor one?" When you compare this with the following two narrations mentioned in Sahih Bukhari, you will realize the truth:

Hazrat Anas (may Allah be pleased with him) says:

"You do actions which are smaller in your eyes than a hair while we considered them during the time of the Prophet (peace be upon him) to be destructive sins." (Destructive sins mean deadly sins)

Ibn Masud (may Allah be pleased with him) says:

"The believer sees his sins as if he is sitting under a mountain which he fears will fall on him, and the wicked person sees his sins as a fly that passes over his nose and he dismisses it with his hand."

Does such a person still not realize the importance of the matter when they read the following hadith of the Prophet (peace be upon him):

"Beware of belittling sins, for their example is like a people who camped in the bottom of a valley, then one brought a stick, and another brought a stick, until they gathered enough to cook their bread. And indeed, belittling sins, when its doer is taken to account, will destroy him." (In another narration): "Beware of belittling sins, for they accumulate on a person until they destroy him."

And the scholars say that:

With minor sins, sometimes there is a lack of shame, carelessness, lack of fear of Allah Almighty, and belittling of the sin itself, and all these things can turn it into a major sin. In fact, they say that when a minor sin is done repeatedly, it does not remain minor, and if one seeks forgiveness for a major sin, it does not remain major.

We say: Do not look at the smallness of the sin but look at the greatness of the One you are disobeying. Such people will benefit, God willing, who feel the greatness of their sins and shortcomings. They are neither indifferent to their misguidance nor persistent in their false beliefs. These are the people who believe in the saying of Allah Almighty.

Inform My servants that indeed, I am the Forgiving, the Merciful. (Al-Hijr: 49) Just as they believe in the saying of Allah Almighty. And that My punishment is the painful punishment. (Al-Hijr: 50) The conditions of repentance and the things that complete it

Repentance is a very significant term, whose implications are very deep. It is not like what most people think, that just saying the word "repentance" with the tongue while continuing to commit sins suffices. Just consider this saying of Allah Almighty: And seek forgiveness of your Lord and then repent to Him. And you will realize that repentance is something additional to seeking forgiveness. And because it is a significant matter, it has some conditions. Scholars have derived these conditions from verses and hadiths. Some of them are as follows:

1. The sin must be abandoned immediately and completely.
2. One must feel regret for the past sin.
3. One must make a firm resolution not to commit that sin in the future.
4. The rights of those who were wronged must be restored, either by seeking their forgiveness or by making amends.

The blind person showed the way

I was thirty years old when my wife gave birth to my first son... I still cannot forget that night... because I stayed up late at a rest house with my friends, where we remained engaged in pointless conversations until late at night. And it was not just that; it also included gossiping about others, backbiting, disparaging people unjustly and unlawfully, and mocking them... I was often the one making others laugh... I was mostly the one who gossiped and backbit, and my friends would laugh and giggle upon hearing it... I still remember that night when I had made them laugh a lot.

I had a peculiar talent for imitating others. I would alter my voice to make it closer to that of the person I was mocking.

Yes! I kept ridiculing everyone.

Moreover, even my own friends were not spared from my hands, to the extent that some people started to avoid me, so they could remain safe from the arrows and daggers of my tongue.

I remember clearly that night when I mocked a beggar begging in the market and did something extremely dangerous by putting my foot in front of him, causing him to stumble and fall. The entire market echoed with my loud laughter... and as usual, I returned home very late that night.

What did I see? My wife was sitting waiting for me, and her condition appeared extremely pitiable. In a trembling and broken voice, she addressed me: "Rasheed! Where have you been?"

I mocked her saying: "I was not on Mars, I was with my friends." The signs of exhaustion and weakness were clearly visible on her. She said with a choked voice:

"Rasheed! I am in a lot of pain. It seems that the time for the child's delivery is very near."

As she said this, a silent tear rolled down her cheek. At that moment, I began to feel that I had been extremely negligent about my wife, whereas it was my duty to take care of her... especially since she was in the ninth month.

I immediately took her to the hospital, and she was admitted to the maternity ward's labor room, where she endured hours of pain and suffering.

I was waiting impatiently for the birth of the baby, to the extent that I became exhausted from waiting... and I went back home... On my way back, I left my phone number with the staff so they could give me the good news.

An hour later, the phone rang; when I picked up the receiver, the hospital staff gave me the news that a flower had bloomed in your courtyard, which I had already decided to name "Salim."

I rushed to the hospital, and upon arrival, I asked the staff for my wife's room... They told me to first meet with the lady doctor who was in charge of the delivery.

I shouted, "Which doctor should I meet? I want to see my son 'Salim' first."

They said, "First meet the doctor."

I entered the doctor's room... and this lady began to talk about hardships and trials and the importance of accepting Allah's written destiny and decree with happiness and contentment. Then she told me that upon closely examining both of my son's eyes, it seemed that he might be deprived of the blessing of sight and is likely blind!

I lowered my head. I was trying to hold back my tears... And at the same time, I remembered that blind beggar whom I had knocked down and made people laugh at in the market.

SubhanAllah! It is true: "As you do, so you shall receive." And "You reap what you sow."

For a moment, my tongue was paralyzed with the intensity of grief... I couldn't figure out what to say... Then I remembered my wife and son. I thanked the doctor for her gentle advice and kind words and went to see my wife...

My wife was not saddened... She had faith in Allah's decree and was content with it. She had always advised me to refrain from mocking others... She always used to tell me not to backbite people... and not to spread gossip about anyone.

After discharging my wife, we left the hospital and Salim was also in our arms.

The reality was that I had never cared for this son of mine... I acted as if he wasn't even present in the house.

Whenever he cried loudly for some reason, I would flee from the bedroom and go sleep in the drawing room... However, my wife took great care of him and loved him dearly... As for me, I didn't hate him, but I couldn't love him either... Salim grew up... Now he had started to crawl and walk.

His crawling was quite strange as well... He was approaching one year old, and when he started trying to walk, we faced a new revelation:

not only was he blind, but he was also lame... Now he felt like an even heavier burden to me.

After that, my wife gave birth to two other sons, Umar and Khalid... Years passed by... Salim grew up, and his two brothers also grew up... I did not like staying at home... Instead, I always spent more time outside the house with my friends.

The reality is that I had become a toy in their hands... My wife never lost hope in correcting me... She always prayed for my guidance and improvement and never expressed anger at my negligent behavior.

However, whenever she felt my negligence towards Salim and saw my love and affection for the other children... she would become distressed and melancholic about this duality... Salim continued to grow, and along with him, my sorrow also increased. When my wife requested that I enroll Salim in a special school for disabled children, I did not refuse her... I didn't even feel the passage of years; the days and nights continued in the same routine. Working, sleeping, eating, and aimlessly staying awake at nights.

One Friday, I woke up from sleep at eleven in the morning... To me, it still seemed very early.

I was invited to a wedding party... I put on new, beautiful clothes, fragranced myself with perfume, and as I was passing through the corridor to go outside, I saw Salim crying in a very heart-wrenching manner... This sight made me stop. It was the first time since Salim's childhood that his crying had attracted my attention. Ten years had passed, and I had never paid any attention to him... This time, I tried to ignore him, but I couldn't bear it. I was in the room, hearing his crying and calling out to his mother.

I turned my attention towards him... I went closer to him and said: "Salim! Why are you crying?"

When he heard my voice, he stopped crying, and when he realized I was close to him, he started moving his small hands around to feel his surroundings... What happened to him?...

I realized that he was trying to move away from me!! And it seemed as if he was silently saying, "Father! Now you are aware of my existence? Where were you during the past ten years?"

I followed him as he entered his room... At first, he refused to tell me why he was crying, but when I expressed my affection and love and gently asked him the reason, he began to explain why he was crying. I listened carefully to his words and was inwardly shedding tears of blood.

Do you know what he said was the reason for his crying?

The reason was that his brother Umar, who used to take him to the mosque, was late in reaching him. Today, since it was Friday... he began to fear that he might not get a place in the front row for the Friday prayer... He then started calling Umar and his mother again and again... but there was no one near him to hear his voice... I began to see the tears falling from his sightless eyes... and I could not bear to hear the rest of his conversation... I placed my hand over his mouth... and said to him:

"O Salim! Are you crying because of this?"

He said: "Yes!"

I forgot my friends and companions... I forgot the wedding invitation as well... and spontaneously I said:

"Salim! Don't be sad... Do you know who will take you to the mosque today?"

He said with great innocence: "Certainly, only Umar will take me to the mosque... but the problem is that he always gets late."

I said: "No, Salim! Today, Umar will not take you; I will take you to the mosque myself."

Salim was stunned upon hearing this... He could not believe it. He thought I might be joking with him... He was silent for a moment and then started crying again... I wiped away the tears falling from his eyes with my hands... and then took his hand.

I decided to take him to the mosque in the car... but he refused to get into the car, saying:

"The mosque is nearby, and I want to walk to the mosque on my own feet, because every step earns a reward."

I swear by Allah! This is what he said... I don't know when was the last time I entered the mosque, but this was the first time I felt fear and shame upon entering the mosque. This fear and shame were due to the neglects I had committed over the past years... The mosque was crowded with worshippers yet I found a place in the front row for Salim.

We both listened to the Friday sermon together, and he prayed the Friday prayer beside me... After the prayer, Salim asked me for the Quran... I was quite surprised... I wondered to myself how he, being blind, would recite the Quran?

I was almost going to ignore his request, but then, to keep him happy, I handed him the Quran so his feelings would not be hurt... Now he asked me to open the Quran and find Surah Al-Kahf... I started flipping through the pages... sometimes looking at the list of surahs.

Eventually, I found Surah Al-Kahf... He took the Quran from my hands... placed it in front of him... and began reciting Surah Al-Kahf while his eyes were closed.

Oh Allah!! He had memorized the entire Surah Al-Kahf by heart!! Now I was deeply ashamed... I also took the Mushaf in my hand... My joints were trembling.

I recited the Quran. And I recited it well that day... and prayed to my Lord to forgive my sins and guide me to the right path... Now I could not control my heart, and I started crying like a child... There were still some people in the mosque who were praying the Sunnah prayers after the Friday prayers... As I tried to control my crying due to embarrassment, my crying turned into sobs and gasps... I lost awareness of myself when I felt a tiny hand searching for my face... and then it wiped my tears.

It was Salim... I took him in my arms and held him to my chest. I looked at him and silently said... You are not blind... Rather, it is I who am blind, drawn to these sinful and corrupt friends who were dragging me towards the fire of hell.

When we, father and son, returned home from the mosque, I saw that my wife was very worried about Salim. But now her worry had turned into a stream of tears overwhelmed by joy because she had found out that I had also performed the Friday prayer with Salim. From that day I have never missed a congregational prayer in the mosque. I left my bad society and severed ties with corrupt friends. Instead, I now have friendships with good and pious people whom I met in the mosque. After mingling with them, I experienced the true sweetness and pleasure of faith. I learned from them those things that worldly affairs had kept me heedless of.

I have never missed a dhikr or study circle, nor have I ever missed the Witr or Tahajjud prayers. In just one month, I completed the entire Quran several times. I always keep my tongue moist with the remembrance of Allah, hoping that Allah may forgive my previous distance from religion, my mockery of people, and my derision of them.

I have realized that I am now much closer to my family than before. The fearful and scared looks that used to reflect from my wife's eyes have disappeared. My son Salim's lips always carry a smile… those who see him think that he must have received the whole world and all its riches. I am immensely grateful to Allah for these blessings.

One day, some of my companions planned a journey to distant and backward areas to invite people to the correct creed and to spread religious teachings based on the pure Quran and Sunnah. Initially, I was a bit hesitant.

Then I prayed Salat al-Istikhara for guidance and also consulted my wife. I expected her to refuse. But the situation was completely the opposite! She was very happy to hear my intention. In fact, with expressions of joy and delight, she encouraged and supported me for this journey. Previously, she used to see me setting out on sinful and morally corrupt trips without consulting her.

Now I went to my beloved Salim. I told him that I was going on a journey. He embraced me with his tiny hands and bid me farewell with joy and cheerfulness. I spent three and a half months away from home. During this time, whenever I got a chance, I called my wife and also talked to my sons. I missed all of them very much. But alas! I missed Salim the most. I longed to hear his voice. He was the only one who, since I had embarked on this journey, had not spoken to me.

When I called, sometimes he was at the madrasa and sometimes at the mosque. Whenever I expressed my desire and eagerness to meet and talk to Salim, my wife would burst into joy and her laughter would overflow with happiness. Except for my last call. This time, I did not hear the expected sound of her laughter. Her voice sounded a bit altered.

I told her to give my regards to Salim. She said, "Insha'Allah." And then she fell silent. Eventually, I completed my journey and returned home. I knocked on the door of my house, secretly hoping that Salim would be the one to open it.

But the one who opened the door was my son Khalid, who was not even four years old. I embraced him in my arms, and he happily called out, "Abu, Abu!" I don't know why I began to feel a sense of suffocation in my heart after entering the house. I sought refuge from the devil's harm. I recited, "A'uzu billahi min ash-shaytan ir-rajim." Meanwhile, my wife was approaching me. Her face looked somewhat changed. She was showing a forced happiness. I looked at her carefully and then asked her: "What happened to you?"

She said, "Nothing at all." Then I remembered Salim.

I asked, "Where is Salim?"

She lowered her head and did not answer.

However, her eyes overflowed with tears due to the intensity of her grief, and warm tears flowed down her cheeks. I shouted, "Salim!! Where is Salim?"

At that moment, I could only hear my son Khalid's voice, saying in his tiny, babyish voice, "Papa! Salim has gone to heaven. Allah be praised!!"

My wife could not bear the sight and burst into tears. She was close to collapsing from the intensity of her sorrow. I then came out of the room.

Later, I found out that two weeks before my return, Salim had a severe fever. My wife took him to the hospital. The fever worsened and showed no sign of subsiding. Eventually, due to the fever, his soul departed from his body. "Inna lillahi wa inna ilayhi raji'un."

Salim passed away. He was disabled and physically blind, but he showed the way to a real blind person like me!

Some scholars have also detailed some other conditions for sincere repentance, which we will list here with some examples.

First: The sin must be abandoned solely for the sake of Allah Almighty. There should be no other reason. For example, if one leaves the sin only because he does not have the ability to commit the sin again, or if he leaves it because he fears people's opinions, then we cannot call such a person repentant.

Similarly, if a person leaves a sin because it affects their status or reputation among people, or sometimes because they have to leave their occupation, they are not considered repentant.

We also cannot call someone repentant who leaves a sin to protect their health and strength. For instance, if someone avoids adultery and indecency due to the fear of contracting filthy contagious diseases, or because such acts would weaken their body and memory, they are not truly repentant.

Nor can we consider someone repentant who stopped stealing because they found no way to enter the house or could not open the safe, or feared the guard or policeman.

We also cannot call someone repentant who did not take a bribe because they were afraid they would be handed over to the anti-corruption department.

And one cannot be called repentant who leaves alcohol and intoxicants only because they could not acquire them due to their sincerity.

Similarly, one cannot be called repentant who becomes incapable of committing a sin due to an external factor, such as a person who cannot speak due to paralysis or a fornicator who no longer has the ability to engage in intercourse, or a thief who has encountered an accident that has disabled them.

Rather, for a person to be considered repentant, it is essential to completely abandon the sin and the desire for disobedience, and to regret past actions. The Prophet Muhammad (peace be upon him) said: "Regret is repentance."

And Allah Almighty has placed those who desire to commit the sin but are incapacitated verbally in the same position as those who act upon their desires. Consider what the Prophet Muhammad (peace be upon him) has said:

In this world, there are four types of people: The first is one who is given both wealth and knowledge by Allah. He fears his Lord, maintains family ties, and knows the rights of Allah. This person is in the highest rank. The second is one who is given knowledge but not wealth. He is sincere in his intentions and says, "If I had wealth, I would do such and such." He will be rewarded according to his intention. Both of these are equal in reward. The third is one who is given wealth but not knowledge. He uses his wealth without knowledge, does not fear Allah, does not maintain family ties, and does not understand the rights of Allah. This person is in the worst rank. The fourth is one who is given neither wealth nor knowledge. He says, "If I had wealth, I would do such and such." Such a person will be treated according to his intention, and both are equal in the burden of sin.

Second: The repentant must understand the gravity and harm of the sin thoroughly. True repentance is such that when recalling past sins, one should not feel any pleasure or delight associated with them, nor should they wish to commit the sin again in the future. Ibn Qayyim (may Allah have mercy on him) has outlined several harms of sins in his books "Al-Daa' wa al-Dawaa'" and "Al-Fawaid," including:

- Deprivation of knowledge

- Heart's harshness

- The burden of actions

- Weakness of the body

- Deprivation of obedience

- Loss of blessings

- Lack of success

- Tightness in the chest

- Emergence of evil

- Becoming habitual in sins

- Loss of honor with Allah and people

- Curses on the livestock

- Garment of humiliation

- Sealing of the heart

- Being subject to curses

- Rejection of supplications

- Corruption on land and sea

- Loss of zeal

- Loss of modesty

- Decline of blessings

- Descent of revulsions

- Imposing fear in the disobedient's heart

- Becoming a captive of Satan

- Bad end and punishment in the Hereafter.

If someone becomes aware of these harms of sins, it will keep them entirely away from sins.

Then, there are some who, after leaving one act of disobedience, fall into another. Some reasons for this include:

1. They believe their sin is minor.

2. Their inclination towards the new sin is stronger and more appealing.

3. Conditions and circumstances for the new sin are more accessible compared to the previous sin, which requires preparation and resources.

4. Their friends and companions persist in committing the sin, making it difficult for them to leave.

5. Sometimes, the specific sin gives them a certain status among their peers, and losing that status is burdensome. Thus, they continue committing the sin, similar to some leaders of corrupt groups, or like the poet Abu Nuwas who, when advised by the preacher-poet Abu al-Atahiya to abandon sin and stop supporting immorality, responded with:

"O Abu al-Atahiya, do you think I will abandon this frivolity? Do you think I would ruin the status I have among these people by adopting asceticism?"

Third: The repentant should quickly turn towards repentance. Delaying repentance itself becomes another sin that requires repentance.

Fourth: The repentant should fear defects in their repentance. They should not assume that their repentance is certainly accepted, nor should they become confident in themselves and neglect the measures of Allah's decree.

Fifth: If possible, one should fulfill any rights of Allah that have been missed, such as not paying Zakat in the past, because the poor also have a right to it.

Sixth: One should abandon the place of disobedience. If there is a risk that remaining there might lead them back to sin, they should leave.

Seventh: One should also avoid those who assist in committing sins. (This, along with the previous point, is derived from the hadith about the one who killed a hundred people, which will be mentioned later.)

Allah Almighty says:

"Friends on that Day will be enemies to one another, except for the righteous." (Surah Az-Zukhruf: 67)

On the Day of Judgment, bad companions will curse one another. Therefore, O repentant person, if you are unable to invite them to righteousness, then it is necessary for you to separate from them, distance yourself, boycott them, and be cautious that Satan does not make you return to them. If Satan invites you back, he may beautify their invitation and make you believe that you are too weak to stand against them. Many have relapsed into sin because of past associations.

Eighth: If one possesses forbidden items, they should be disposed of. For example, intoxicants, musical instruments like the oud and flute, pictures, forbidden films, obscene stories, and dramas should be destroyed, discarded, or burned.

To ensure that repentance remains steadfast, it is essential for the repentant person to abandon all the prerequisites of sinfulness; otherwise, the benefits of repentance will not be realized. Many cases are reported where the remaining forbidden items led to the failure of repentance and deviation after guidance. We pray to Allah for steadfastness.

Ninth: One should choose righteous friends instead of bad ones who can help in maintaining the sincerity of repentance. One should join gatherings of knowledge and remembrance and engage in beneficial activities so that Satan does not find a way through past memories.

Tenth: The body, which was nourished by forbidden earnings, should now be used in the path of Allah and adopt lawful means so that pure sustenance is produced in the future.

Eleventh: Repentance should be done before the soul reaches the throat (Ghargharah) and before the sun rises from the west. Ghargharah refers to the sound that comes from the throat when the soul is departing. The goal is that repentance should be made before the Judgment Day. The Prophet Muhammad (peace be upon him) said:

"Whoever repents to Allah before the soul reaches the throat, Allah accepts their repentance."

The Prophet Muhammad (peace be upon him) also said:

"Whoever repents before the sun rises from the west, Allah accepts their repentance."

Once there was a king

Some people have hearts eager to follow the path of guidance. But pride and arrogance prevent them from adhering to the commands of religion. Yes! Their pride and arrogance come in the way of keeping their clothes above their ankles and growing beards to oppose the polytheists. To them, their false dignity and outward beauty are more desirable and beloved than the obedience and submission to their Lord.

A similar case is with some women. They show laziness in matters of the Shariah veil and covering. In their view, they complete their adornment and enhance their appearance and beauty. Some women disobey their Lord by plucking their eyebrows and wearing tight and revealing clothes. When advised, they become rebellious and display arrogance. Whereas a person cannot enter paradise who has even a tiny bit of pride and arrogance in their heart, let alone if this pride not only exists but also obstructs the acceptance of truth.

One of the kings from the tribe of Bani Ghassan was a king named Jabala bin Ayham. The light of faith entered his heart and he became a Muslim. He sent a letter to the Leader of the Believers, Umar Farooq (Allah be pleased with him), in which he sought permission to present himself before him. Umar Farooq (Allah be pleased with him) and all the companions and followers were very happy to hear this. Accordingly, Umar (Allah be pleased with him) wrote a letter to him granting permission to present himself. Along with this, he also stated, "You have all the same rights that we all Muslims have, and the same duties and responsibilities are imposed upon you that are upon all of us."

Jabala came with his tribe of five hundred horsemen. When he approached Madinah, he wore his royal robe made of golden threads. He put on his crown studded with diamonds and jewels. He ordered his soldiers to wear luxurious garments. Then he entered Madinah with his entourage. All the people of Madinah came out to see them, even women and children were eager to see this sight.

When the King of Ghassan, Jabala, reached Umar Farooq (Allah be pleased with him), he welcomed him and seated him close to him. When the season of Hajj arrived, Umar Farooq (Allah be pleased with him) performed the Hajj. Jabala also set out for Hajj with him. While he was performing Tawaf, a poor man from Bani Fazara accidentally stepped on Jabala's robe. Jabala, in anger, looked at him and slapped him hard on his face, breaking his nose. The poor man from Bani Fazara became very angry.

He complained about Jabala's act to Umar Farooq (Allah be pleased with him). Umar Farooq (Allah be pleased with him) sent for him and asked:

"O Jabala! Why did you slap your brother during the Tawaf? You even broke his nose?"

He replied with full pride and arrogance:

"He stepped on my robe. If it weren't for the sanctity and holiness of the Kaaba, I would have cut off his neck."

Umar Farooq (Allah be pleased with him) said:

"Now that you have admitted your act, you must do one of two things: either appease him in any way and make him withdraw his claim, or you will be subjected to Qisas (retribution), and this poor and needy Fazari man will slap you on your face."

Jabala said: "He will take revenge on me, while I am a king, and he is a street pauper?"

Umar Farooq (Allah be pleased with him) said:

"O Jabala! Islam has given you and him equal rights and duties. If anyone has superiority over another, it is only due to piety."

Jabala then said:

"Then I will become a Christian."

Umar Farooq (Allah be pleased with him) said:

"The Prophet (PBUH) said:

'Whoever changes his religion, kill him.' (Sahih al-Bukhari, Hadith No. 6524).

If you become a Christian, I will cut off your head."

Jabala said:

"O Leader of the Believers! Grant me a respite until tomorrow to think."

Umar Farooq (Allah be pleased with him) said: "Go! You are given respite."

When night fell, Jabala fled from Makkah with his companions. He reached Constantinople and became a Christian there.

When a long time passed living there, the period of pleasures ended and the time of regrets came. Then he remembered his days of being a Muslim. He longed for the sweetness of prayer and fasting. He regretted abandoning the religion of Islam. Overwhelmed with remorse for associating partners with Allah, he began to cry and, consumed by regret, he composed some verses in which he expressed his shame for becoming an apostate.

The nobles converted to Christianity out of the shame of a slap,

And had they been patient with that slap, there would have been no harm in it.

Arrogance and pride overwhelmed me from it,

And I sold the sound eye for a squinted one because of it (i.e., I abandoned Islam and accepted Christianity).

Oh, I wish my mother had never given birth to me, alas! I should have accepted what Umar (Allah be pleased with him) said to me.

Oh, I wish I had been herding camels in a barren desert and had been a prisoner of Banu Rabi'ah or Mudar.

Oh, I wish I had the lowest subsistence in Sham, sitting among my people blind and deaf.

But he remained steadfast in the Christian faith and died in that state. Yes, he died in a state of disbelief, for he was arrogant in submitting to the Sharia of Allah, the Lord of the Worlds. (Al-Bidaya wa'l-Nihaya: 8/ 62)

A Great Woman's Repentance

A Ghamidiyyah woman came to the Prophet Muhammad (peace be upon him) and said: "O Messenger of Allah! I have committed adultery. Purify me." The Prophet (peace be upon him) sent her away. The next day she came back and said: "O Messenger of Allah! Why do you keep sending me away? Perhaps you are sending me back in the same way as you did with Ma'iz." By Allah, I am pregnant." The Prophet (peace be upon him) said: "No, go until you give birth to the child."

The narrator says that when the woman's child was born, she came with the child wrapped in a piece of cloth and said: "This is the child I have delivered." The Prophet (peace be upon him) said to her: "Go, nurse the child until you wean him."

Then, when she had weaned the child, she came with the child holding a piece of bread and said: "O Messenger of Allah! I have weaned the child, and now he has started eating." The Prophet (peace be upon him) entrusted the child to one of his companions and then ordered her stoning. Thus, a pit was dug up to her chest and she was stoned to death. Khalid bin Al-Walid (may Allah be pleased with him) stepped forward and struck the woman's head with a stone. The blood splashed onto Khalid's face, so he cursed her, which the Prophet Muhammad (peace be upon him) heard. The Prophet (peace be upon him) said to Khalid (may Allah be pleased with him): "Hold on, Khalid! By Him in Whose Hand is my soul, she has repented a repentance if it were divided among seventy of the people of Madinah, it would suffice them." Khalid! What is this? By Him in Whose Hand is my soul, if the tax collector had repented like this woman, he would also be forgiven."

In another narration, it is mentioned that Umar (may Allah be pleased with him) said: "The Prophet Muhammad (peace be upon him) stoned the woman and then he performed the funeral prayer for her. The Prophet (peace be upon him) said: 'She has repented a repentance if it were distributed among seventy of the people of Madinah, it would be enough for them. Is there anything better than that she has given her soul for Allah, the Mighty and Majestic?'"

Repentance Erases Previous Sins

Sometimes, a person says: "I want to repent, but who can guarantee that if I repent, Allah will forgive me? I am eager to follow the path of steadfastness, but my consciousness puts me in doubt. If I were certain that Allah would surely forgive me, I would definitely repent." The response to this is that the feeling of doubt you are experiencing was also felt by some of the companions of the Prophet Muhammad (peace be upon him).

And if you carefully consider the following two narrations, insha'Allah your doubts will be dispelled.

Imam Muslim (may Allah have mercy on him) narrates the story of the conversion of Amr bin Aas (may Allah be pleased with him):

Then, when Allah placed love for Islam in my heart, I came to the Prophet (peace be upon him) and said: "Extend your right hand so that I can pledge allegiance." The Prophet (peace be upon him) extended his hand, which I took in mine. The Prophet (peace be upon him) said: "O Amr! What is your matter?" I said: "I want to make a condition." The Prophet (peace be upon him) asked: "What condition?" I said: "That Allah would forgive me." The Prophet (peace be upon him) said: "Do you not know, O Amr, that Islam obliterates what came before it, and migration obliterates what came before it, and pilgrimage obliterates what came before it?"

Narration by Imam Muslim:

Imam Muslim narrated from Ibn Abbas (may Allah be pleased with both of them) that: "Some polytheists had committed many murders and many acts of adultery, then they came to Muhammad (peace be upon him) and said: 'The One you speak of and the thing you call for is good. I wish you would tell us what the expiation for our deeds is.' Then Allah revealed this verse:

[And those who do not invoke with Allah another deity or kill the soul which Allah has forbidden, except by right, and do not commit unlawful sexual intercourse. And whoever should do that shall meet a penalty.] (Al-Furqan: 68)

And this verse was revealed:

[Say, 'O My servants who have harmed yourselves by your own selves, do not despair of the mercy of Allah. Indeed, Allah forgives all sins. Indeed, He is the Forgiving, the Merciful.] (Az-Zumar: 53)

Will Allah forgive me?

And sometimes you say: "I want to repent, but my sins are so many that there is no type of immorality I have left out. I have committed every sin imaginable and unimaginable, and I have committed so many sins over this long period that I wonder if it is possible for Allah to forgive them all?"

O my respected brother! I say to you that this difficulty is not unique to you but is experienced by many who repent. In this regard, I present the example of a young man who once asked: "I have been involved in disobedience and sins since a young age, and I am now only seventeen years old. My list of small and large sins, including various types, is very long. I have committed these acts with people of all types, including even a young female, and I have stolen several times. Now I have repented before Allah, the Mighty and Majestic. I perform the night prayer and fast every Monday and Thursday, and I read the Qur'an after the Fajr prayer. Is there room for repentance for me?"

We, the people of Islam, refer to the Book and the Sunnah for seeking rulings and solutions to issues. And when we turn to the Book of Allah, we find His command:

[Say, 'O My servants who have harmed yourselves by your own selves, do not despair of the mercy of Allah. Indeed, Allah forgives all sins. Indeed, He is the Forgiving, the Merciful. And turn in repentance to your Lord and submit to Him.] (Az-Zumar: 54, 55)

This is the clear and proper response to the mentioned difficulty, so clear that no further explanation is needed.

As for the feeling that sins are so numerous that it is unlikely Allah would forgive them, this stems from a lack of belief in the vastness of Allah's mercy. This is the first issue.

The second issue is a deficiency in faith regarding Allah's ability to forgive all sins.

The third issue is a weakness in hope, which is a crucial aspect of the heart's actions.

The fourth issue is that even if repentance is accepted, there might be a lack of power to erase the sins.

Now, let us address each of these issues:

For the first issue, Allah's statement is sufficient:

[And My mercy encompasses all things.] (Al-A'raf: 156)

For the second issue, the following Hadith Qudsi is sufficient. Allah says:

Allah, the Most High, says: "Whoever knows that I have the power to forgive sins, I will forgive him, and I do not care, as long as he does not associate partners with Me."

REGARDING THE THIRD issue, the following great Hadith Qudsi provides the remedy:

"O son of Adam! As long as you call upon Me and have hope in Me, I will forgive you for whatever you have done, and I do not care. O son of Adam! If your sins were to reach the height of the sky, then you sought forgiveness from Me, I would forgive you, and I do not care. O son of Adam! If you came to Me with sins as great as the earth and met Me without associating anything with Me, I would bring you as much forgiveness as the earth."

Regarding the fourth issue, the Prophet (peace be upon him) said:

"The one who repents from sin is like one who has no sin."

For someone who thinks their sins are so numerous that Allah would not forgive them, we present the Hadith of "the killer of a hundred men":

The Killer of One Hundred Men

Abu Sa'id al-Khudri (may Allah be pleased with him) said that the Prophet (peace be upon him) said: "Among the people before you was a man who killed ninety-nine people. He asked the people, 'Who is the most knowledgeable person on earth?' They pointed him to a monk. He went to him and said, 'I have killed ninety-nine people. Is there any repentance for me?' The monk said, 'No.' So he killed the monk and completed the hundred. Then he asked the people, 'Who is the most knowledgeable person on earth?' They pointed him to a scholar. He went to the scholar and said, 'I have killed a hundred people. Is there any repentance for me?' The scholar said, 'Yes, there is nothing between you and repentance. Go to such-and-such a land where people worship Allah, and join these people in their worship of Allah. Do not return to your own land; it is a bad place.' So he set out for that land. He had covered only half the distance when death came to him. Now the angels of mercy and punishment disputed about him. The angels of mercy said, 'This man had repented sincerely and had started going towards Allah's path.' The angels of punishment said, 'He never did a good deed.' Then an angel appeared in the form of a man, and they made him an arbitrator. He said, 'Measure the distance between the two lands. The angel of the land he was closest to will take his soul.' They measured and found that he was closer to the land he was heading towards. So the angels of mercy took him."

In another authentic narration:

They measured and found that the land of the righteous people was a span closer, so he was counted among the righteous people.

In another authentic narration:

Allah commanded the land to move away from him and commanded the land towards which he was heading to come closer. When they measured, the land of the righteous people was found to be a span closer, so he was forgiven.

Indeed, what could possibly be a barrier to this person's repentance? Therefore, O one who intends to repent, reflect whether your sins are greater than those of this person whom Allah forgave. Why then despair?

O my Muslim brother! The matter is even greater. Consider Allah's statement:

[And those who do not invoke with Allah another deity or kill the soul which Allah has forbidden, except by right, and do not commit unlawful sexual intercourse. And whoever should do that shall meet a penalty. Their punishment will be doubled for them on the Day of Resurrection, and they will abide eternally therein humbled. Except for those who repent, believe and do righteous work. For them Allah will replace their evil deeds with good. And ever is Allah Forgiving and Merciful.] (Al-Furqan: 68-70)

And also Allah's statement: "For them Allah will replace their evil deeds with good." With this it becomes clear to you that this is a great favor from Allah. Scholars say that this change is of two types:

The first type is that bad qualities will be changed into good qualities. For example, shirk (polytheism) will be replaced by faith, fornication by chastity and purity, lying by truthfulness, and treachery by trustworthiness, etc.

And the second type is that the sins they committed will be replaced by good deeds on the Day of Resurrection. Reflect on Allah's statement: "For them Allah will replace their evil deeds with good." Allah did not say that every evil will be turned into a good deed. It is possible that they may be less in number, equal, or more, and this change will be according to the sincerity of the repentant and the perfection of his repentance. Can you see any favor greater than this?

At this point, a repentant might ask: When I was astray, I did not perform prayers and was outside the Islamic community, at that time I also did some good deeds. Will they be counted after repentance or will they be wasted?

And the answer is narrated by Urwah bin Zubair that Hakim bin Hizam told him that he asked the Messenger of Allah (peace be upon him), "O Messenger of Allah! What do you think about the charities I used to give and the emancipation of slaves and maintaining kinship ties I did in the pre-Islamic period? Will I be rewarded for those deeds?" The Messenger of Allah (peace be upon him) said, "You accepted Islam with all the good deeds you had done before."

It means that after repentance, sins will be forgiven, and the bad deeds will be turned into good deeds, and the good deeds done in the period of ignorance will remain for the doer. So, what is left after that?

A preacher in a dance club

There was a small mosque in our neighborhood, where an elderly and very great preacher and propagator of religion used to lead people in prayer. He had spent his entire life leading people in prayer and teaching them about religion. He noticed that the number of worshippers was decreasing day by day. He kept a close eye on the worshippers and took great care of this matter. He considered them his children.

One day, this pious man turned to the worshippers and said: What has happened to most people? Especially the youth, they neither come near the mosque nor know the way to the mosque? The worshippers present in the mosque replied to the Imam: People are engrossed in dance halls and places of amusement. The Imam said: Dance halls!! What are these dance halls?

One person said: A dance hall is in the form of a hall with a wooden stage. Young maidens climb on it and dance, and people sit around and watch them dance. Hearing this, the words "I seek refuge in Allah" came out of the Imam's mouth, and he asked in great astonishment:

Those people who watch the dance of these young girls, are they Muslims? People said: Yes!

The elderly respected Sheikh said with great innocence: "There is no power nor strength except with Allah," and then he began to say very seriously:

It is obligatory upon us to advise and admonish them.

People said:

O respected Sheikh! Will you go to the dance hall and advise and admonish them?

He said: Yes!

Then he got up and went out of the mosque. As he was going, he kept saying: Come with us to that dance hall (dance club).

People tried to dissuade him from his intention. They informed the Sheikh that upon going there, we will all face the ridicule and mockery of those people, and we will have to endure distress and hardship.

The Imam said:

Are we of a higher rank than our Prophet Muhammad (peace be upon him)?

Then the Sheikh took the hand of one person from the worshippers and said: Show me the address of the dance hall. The Sheikh kept walking and continued to move forward with full sincerity and steadfastness until he reached the dance hall. The owner of the dance club saw them coming from afar. He thought perhaps these people were going somewhere to give a lecture or lesson. When they reached the dance hall, he was greatly surprised. When they reached the door of the dance club, the owner asked them: What do you people want?

The Sheikh said: We want to give some advice and admonition to the people engrossed in the spectacle in your dance club.

Hearing this, the club owner was very surprised. He stared at them with wide eyes and began to make excuses to avoid agreeing to their request. The Sheikh explained a lot to him, telling him about the great reward and abundant blessings he would receive. But he did not agree. Now the Sheikh started bargaining by offering money in exchange for permission. Finally, he offered him as much money as his total income for one day. The dance club owner agreed on this condition.

But he demanded that they come the next day at the beginning of the daily dance program. The next day came. People gathered in the dance hall. The stage and the entire hall were filled with evils and immorality. Devils surrounded the people in the hall, and they were clapping for them. Suddenly, the curtain dropped. And then when the curtain was raised, what did people see? A dignified Sheikh was sitting on a chair on the stage. Everyone was astonished to see this scene. They were very surprised. Some of them even thought it was part of a comedy skit or a comedic program.

The respected Imam began his speech by first reciting "Bismillah," then praised Allah Almighty. After that, he sent blessings and peace upon the noble Prophet Muhammad (peace be upon him). Then he started to give advice and admonition to the people. People began to look at each other. Some started laughing, and some began to criticize him. There were even some who started mocking the respected Sheikh and hooting at him. He continued with his sermon, paying no attention to their words and actions. Until one person from among the people present stood up. He made the people quiet and demanded that they listen to the elder's words attentively for once. Silence began to spread among the people, and tranquility and calmness began to descend upon their hearts. Until all voices ceased. Apart from the Sheikh's voice, no other sound was heard.

The Sheikh said things they had never heard before. He recited verses from the Quran that could shake mountains. He presented the sayings of the Prophet (peace be upon him) and gave examples. He mentioned the stories of the repentance of some sinners. And, struggling to control his own tears, he said: O people! You have been living for a long time.

You have committed many disobediences against Allah. Where is the pleasure of those disobediences now?

All those pleasures are gone, but now only the black pages of the record of deeds remain. You will be questioned about these disobediences on the Day of Judgment. Soon a day will come when everything will perish, and only the exalted and omnipotent Allah will remain.

O people! Have you ever examined your deeds and thought about where they are leading you? You cannot endure the fire of this world, while it is only the seventieth part of the fire of Hell (less hot).

People! What has Allah done to you that you have resorted to disobeying Him? Are His blessings and bounties not being bestowed upon you? While only evil arises from you. He bestows His blessings upon you, making you His beloved, and you are determined to become detestable to Him by your disobedience!

The Sheikh was delivering his sermon, and his voice was breaking with overwhelming emotions. Each word uttered by him was coming from the depths of his heart. This is why every word was affecting and clinging to the hearts of the listeners. Now people had started to cry. The respected Sheikh continued his sermon and then began to pray for mercy and forgiveness for all the attendees. And they were humbly saying 'Ameen, Ameen' to his prayers. After this, he stood up from his chair. At that moment, great majesty and dignity were evident in his personality.

The Imam came out from there. All the people followed him out. Yes! All the people. All of them repented at the hands of that elder. They had recognized the secret of their existence in this world and the purpose of their creation. They had also understood that on the Day of Judgment when the records of deeds will be distributed, and sins will have greatly increased, at that time no dance and no pleasure will be of any benefit to them. Moreover, even the owner of the dance club repented and he too was regretful and ashamed of his past actions.

When I sin, what should I do then? Sometimes you say that when I commit a sin, how do I repent for it? What should I do immediately after that sin? Answer: After abandoning the sin, two things should be done: The first is the action of the heart, which is to feel regret and firmly resolve never to do that act again. And this is the result of fear of Allah. The second is the action of the body parts, which is to do various good deeds, one of which is also the prayer of repentance. The explanation is as follows: Hazrat Abu Bakr (may Allah be pleased with him) says that I heard the Messenger of Allah (peace and blessings of Allah be upon him) say: Whoever commits a sin, then stands up and purifies himself, then prays two rak'ahs, then seeks forgiveness from Allah, Allah will forgive him. Then the Prophet (peace be upon him) recited this verse: [And those who, when they commit an immorality or wrong themselves, remember Allah and seek forgiveness for their sins. And who can forgive sins except Allah? And they do not persist in what they have done while they know. (Al-Imran: 135)]

And there are some other authentic narrations in which other attributes of the two rak'ahs that remove these sins are mentioned. Their summary is:

1. Whoever performs ablution and does it well (because the sins are washed away with the water with which the limbs are washed, or they come out with the last drop of water). And doing ablution well means reciting Bismillah before it and then reciting the supplications after it, which are: Ashhadu an la ilaha illallah wahdahu la sharika lahu, wa ashhadu anna Muhammadan abduhu wa rasuluhu (or) Allahumma aj'alni min at-tawwabeen wa aj'alni min al-mutatahhireen (or) Allahumma wa bihamdika ashhadu an la ilaha illa ant, astaghfiruka wa atubu ilayk. I bear witness that there is no god except Allah alone, He

has no partner, and I bear witness that Muhammad is His servant and His messenger. O Allah, make me among those who constantly repent and make me among those who purify themselves. O Allah! With Your praise, I bear witness that there is no deity except You. I seek Your forgiveness and turn to You in repentance. (These supplications are after ablution, and each has great reward.)

2. Stand up and pray two rak'ahs.

3. Keep your heart present and fully attentive in them.

4. Do not get distracted in them.

5. Do not think of anything else in your heart during them.

6. Perform them with proper remembrance and humility.

7. Then seek forgiveness from Allah, and the result will be:

a. His past sins will be forgiven.

b. And Paradise will become obligatory for him.

Then after this, one should do many good and obedient deeds. Don't you see that on the occasion of the Treaty of Hudaybiyyah, when Hazrat Umar (may Allah be pleased with him) realized his mistake, he did many good deeds thereafter to expiate that sin.

Reflect similarly on this authentic hadith in which the Prophet (peace and blessings of Allah be upon him) said: The example of someone who does bad deeds and then does good deeds is like a man who wears a tight coat of mail (an iron garment worn by a fighter), which has choked him. Then he does a good deed, and one ring opens, and he does another good deed, and another ring opens, until he is free and walks on the earth.

In other words, good deeds free the sinner from the bondage of sin and take him to the open field of obedience. And, my brother! The summary of the following instructive story is presented to you:

Hazrat Abdullah bin Masood (may Allah be pleased with him) narrates that a man came to the Prophet (peace and blessings of Allah be upon him) and said: O Messenger of Allah! I met a woman in a garden and did everything with her except for intercourse. I kissed her and embraced her. Now you may deal with me as you wish. The Messenger of Allah (peace and blessings of Allah be upon him) said nothing to him, so the man went away. Hazrat Umar (may Allah be pleased with him) said to him, "Allah had concealed your sin; you should have concealed it yourself." The Messenger of Allah (peace and blessings of Allah be upon him) then looked at him and said, "Call him back to me." The people brought him back to the Prophet (peace and blessings of Allah be upon him), and he recited this verse to him: [And establish prayer at the two ends of the day and at the approach of the night. Indeed, good deeds do away with misdeeds. That is a reminder for those who remember. (Hud: 114)].

Hazrat Mu'adh (may Allah be pleased with him) said ... and in the narration of Hazrat Umar (may Allah be pleased with him) it is said ... O Messenger of Allah! Is this only for him, or is it for all the people? The Prophet (peace and blessings of Allah be upon him) said: Rather, it is for all the people.

The Misguided Old Man

Sometimes it happens that a person recognizes the truth and wants to follow it. But he is deceived by the worldly possessions and remains adamant in sin and disobedience. Yes! Sometimes position and wealth, sometimes power and glory, and sometimes friendships become obstacles in the acceptance of the truth, causing a person to abandon steadfastness in religion and prefer the worldly life. However, the reality is that the Hereafter is better and eternal.

Al-A'sha ibn Qais was a very great and eloquent poet. He had reached old age. He set out from Yamamah in the region of Najd because he wanted to present himself to the Noble Prophet (peace be upon him) and accept Islam. He was riding his mount, driven by great passion and longing to behold the Prophet (peace be upon him), and he was composing and reciting praise in his honor out of intense joy:

"Did your eyes not close all night due to an eye ailment,

And you stayed awake like a snake-bitten person in sleeplessness?"

"O you who ask me where my mount is headed,

Know that it has an appointment with the people of Yathrib."

"A Prophet who sees what you do not see, and his mention,

By my life, has spread far and wide in the land."

"I find that you have not heard the counsel of Muhammad,

The Prophet of Allah, where he advised and testified."

"If you did not depart with the provision of piety,

And after death, you met one who was well-provided."

As he approached the city of Yathrib (Madinah), he was filled with anticipation and continued his journey, eager to meet the Prophet (peace be upon him) and embrace the truth of Islam.

"You will be regretful that you were not like him,

And that you did not prepare for the matter (accountability) as he did."

He continued to traverse the forests and deserts, driven by a passion and longing to see the Prophet (peace be upon him). He was filled with the desire to embrace Islam and was disillusioned with the worship of idols and deities.

When he neared Madinah, some pagans intervened and asked him where he was going. He told them that he was going to present himself to the Prophet (peace be upon him) to accept Islam. The pagans feared that if even this great poet converted, the Prophet (peace be upon him) would gain more strength. They were already troubled by Hassan ibn Thabit (may Allah be pleased with him) with his poetry, and if this renowned Arab poet also converted, their plight would be worsened.

They told him:

"O A'sha! Your religion and the religion of your ancestors is better for you."

He replied clearly:

"No, rather the religion of Muhammad (peace be upon him) is much better, more appropriate, and correct."

The pagans looked at each other and began to consult on how to prevent him from accepting Islam.

They said to him:

"O A'sha! That Prophet declares fornication to be forbidden." He replied:

"I am an old man. I have no need for women anymore."

They tried to sway him by saying that he forbids alcohol. He replied that it impairs a person's mind and he has no need for it. When they saw that he was firmly determined to accept Islam, they resorted to a more dangerous tactic by tempting him with wealth. They said that if he did not convert to Islam and returned to his ancestral religion, they would give him one hundred camels in exchange.

He began to think about the wealth, which was a significant fortune. Satan overcame his reason, and he yielded to the offer of wealth. He responded:

"Yes! I accept your offer of wealth." They gathered one hundred camels for him. He took them and returned to his people with his disbelief. He went ahead with the one hundred camels, delighted with this worldly gain. His mind was preoccupied with the thought that he had amassed wealth and status along with poetic riches, but he forgot that Allah is waiting to strike. He remained adamant in disobedience to Allah for the sake of worldly wealth, even though Allah is the Possessor of all treasures of the heavens and the earth. As he was nearing his home, he fell from his camel, broke his neck, and died on the spot.

"His loss in this world and the Hereafter was destined, indeed, this is the clear loss." [Al-Hajj: 11]

Sarah, My Daughter

The traffic signal is red, and the entire road is packed with cars. Only a few minutes remain until the scheduled meeting time. Curse this traffic signal! If only I were in the first lane, I would have cut through the signal and moved ahead. Seconds seemed to pass very slowly, as if they were minutes or even hours. In my impatience, I kept glancing at my watch and then at the traffic signal. Finally, the green light came on.

I pressed the horn so loudly that it disturbed everyone around me. The cars slowly started moving forward. I overtook the car in front of me. I nearly collided with another car in the chaos. My reckless driving scared other drivers.

I tried to drive faster, but due to the congestion, I couldn't manage it. Time passed, and I missed my appointment. When I arrived at the scheduled location, none of my friends were there. They had all left. Where should I go? I couldn't find an answer to my question.

I took a deep breath from my chest. If only I could find out where they had gone! Now my car was moving very slowly. I was lost in my thoughts when a car horn jolted me back to reality and pulled me out of my mental fog.

I glared at the driver angrily and signaled with my hand for them to stop honking. The world is not going to fly away. Saying this, I forgot the state I was in a few minutes ago. I resolved that I would spend the night at home. It was a good thought. My only daughter is ill. It is better to stay close to her. I parked my car in front of a video center and went inside the shop. I picked out several movies and headed home. I opened the door and called out to my wife to bring tea and nuts like walnuts, almonds, pistachios, and cashews. She entered the room, and as soon as I saw her, I thought to myself:

What a narrow-minded woman she is. She will now say, "Ahmed! Fear Allah." But I am used to these words. My feelings about these remarks have even faded.

But the reality is that she is a very obedient, dutiful, and virtuous wife. For my happiness, she performs every service with dedication. When she entered the room, she had a tray with tea and dry fruits in her hands. Seeing me, she smiled warmly and said, "Surely, you must be exhausted from staying up with your friends, and now you want to spend time at home, don't you?"

I replied, "Yes. Come, sit down."

Her face brightened with joy. She was about to sit down when I rushed to the TV. Within moments, a cacophony of loud and inappropriate music erupted. She bowed her head and said, "Ahmed, fear Allah." With that, she left the room with feelings of regret and shame, as she did not want to listen to the music. The room filled with loud noises—music, shouting, and laughter. I began drinking tea and eating dry fruits, my eyes glued to the TV screen. One video cassette ended, then another. The clock showed that it was three in the morning, approaching the time for Suhoor.

Suddenly, the door handle moved slowly. I yelled, "What do you want?"

There was no reply. The door opened, and my only sick daughter entered the room. The sudden and unexpected nature of this visit left me momentarily speechless. I couldn't utter a word. She approached me, looked at me calmly, and said, "Abu Jan, fear Allah. Abu Jan, fear Allah." After saying this, she left, closing the door behind her.

I called out, "Sara!" But there was no answer.

I got up and ran after her, unable to believe that this was my daughter. I opened the bedroom door and saw that she had already climbed onto the bed and was lying in her mother's lap. It was indeed her. I returned to the TV lounge and turned off the TV. The room echoed with my daughter's voice: "Abu Jan, fear Allah. Abu Jan, fear Allah."

I was overcome with shivers, my body drenched in sweat. I was unsure of what was happening to me. Her voice was all I could hear. Her image was so ingrained in my eyes that I could see nothing else. Her words tore through the curtains that had long covered my heart and mind. Neglecting prayers, disobedience to Allah and His Messenger (peace be upon him), smoking, and watching filthy films—my daughter had shaken me awake from my deep slumber. My heart raced with fear and remorse. In a strange state of helplessness, I collapsed to the ground.

I made a great effort to sleep. But I couldn't succeed. Time passed very quickly. I recalled all the past actions one by one and presented them before myself. But with each thought, I heard my daughter's echoing voice: "Fear Allah. Fear Allah." At that very moment, the call to Fajr prayer rose in the air. My body shivered. Every part of me was trembling. My hands and feet seemed to have developed a tremor. Meanwhile, the muezzin began to repeat these words:

"Prayer is better than sleep."

Unbidden, my tongue uttered: "You are right. Prayer is better than sleep. Oh God, I have slept through the past year. I have been asleep for a long time." Then I got up, performed ablution, and headed to the mosque. I walked to the mosque as if I had never been there before. It felt like the morning breeze was scolding me, as if saying, "Where have you been all this time?"

It seemed as if the birds soaring in the sky were saying, "Welcome to the one who has finally awakened after a long slumber." I entered the mosque, performed two Sunnah prayers before Fajr, and then sat down to recite the Quran. As I recited, my tongue stumbled. It had been a long time since I had last recited. It felt as if the Quran was asking me: "Why have you abandoned me for so many years? Am I not the speech of your Lord?"

I kept reading this verse from Surah Az-Zumar repeatedly and for a long time, in which Allah Almighty said:

"Say, 'O My servants who have harmed yourselves by your own selves, do not despair of the mercy of Allah. Indeed, Allah forgives all sins. Indeed, He is the Forgiving, the Merciful.'" [Az-Zumar: 53]

Amazing! Allah Almighty forgives all sins. How merciful Allah is to us! I wished I could keep reading the Quran. But the muezzin began the Iqamah. For a moment, I remained rooted in my place. Then I moved forward with the people and stood in the row. I felt quite out of place. The prayer was over. I remained in the mosque until the sun rose... Then I returned home.

I opened the bedroom door. I looked at my wife and Sarah. They were both sleeping. I left them asleep and went to work. It was not my habit to leave for work early in the morning. That's why my office colleagues were astonished to see me in the morning. Voices of congratulations started rising from everywhere, but they were more sarcastic and mocking than congratulatory. I ignored their remarks. My eyes were fixed on the door. I was eagerly awaiting Ibrahim's arrival.

He is also a colleague in the office. He has always given me advice. He is a person of very high morals. Good conduct was his nature. Eventually, Ibrahim arrived. I got up from my place and welcomed him. He could hardly believe his eyes. He asked me: "Are you Ahmed?"

I said: "Yes, I am Ahmed."

I pulled his hand and said: "I want to talk to you."

He said: "No problem. We can talk in the office."

I said: "No... let's go and sit in the rest hall." Ibrahim fell silent and listened carefully to my words. I told him the entire story of last night. His eyes welled up with tears, and at the same time, a smile of joy spread across his face. He said to me: "This is light that has illuminated your heart. Do not extinguish it with sins and disobedience."

Although I had not slept all night, today was a day full of vitality and delight. I was engrossed in my work, and a smile played on my face. People coming for work approached me and sought assistance. Some even asked: "What is this joy and activity today?"

I answered: "It is the blessing of performing the Fajr prayer in congregation at the mosque."

Poor Ibrahim. He used to bear most of the workload. I had no concern other than sleeping. But he never showed displeasure at my behavior nor did he ever complain to the higher authorities. He is such a good person. This is indeed a miracle of the faith whose sweetness has settled in the hearts. Most of the duty time passed, and I did not feel any fatigue.

Ibrahim addressed me: "Ahmed! Now you must go home, because you haven't slept since last night. I will take care of the remaining work." I glanced at the clock. Only a few minutes remained until the Zuhr prayer. I decided that I would stay in the office. The muezzin called the azan. I immediately went to the mosque. I found a place in the front row and sat down. I started feeling a lot of regret about the days when I used to run out as soon as it was time for prayer. After the Zuhr prayer, I headed home. On the way, I was engulfed by a strange feeling of worry and anxiety. I wondered about Sarah's condition. I started feeling suffocated. I could not understand what the reason was.

I began to feel as if the journey from the office to home had become very long today. My fear and anxiety increased. I instinctively looked up at the sky and prayed to Allah Almighty to grant my daughter Sarah a complete and immediate recovery.

I reached home. I opened the door and called out to my wife. I received no response. I quickly entered the bedroom. My wife was sitting hunched and crying. Upon seeing me, she immediately stood up and said, crying: Sarah has passed away. I did not understand what she meant. I went to Sarah and held her to my chest. I tried to gather her into my lap, but her hand fell limp towards the ground. Her body had become very cold. The same was the case with her hands and feet. I could not hear her pulse or her breath. I looked at her forehead. A light was shining, as if she were a bright star. I tried to wake her up. I shook her. I shook her vigorously. Her mother cried out "Sarah, Sarah" and said that Sarah had passed away. Then she burst into tears.

I could not believe what I was seeing. It felt as if I were dreaming. Tears began to stream from my eyes and I started sobbing. I looked at her beautiful face and soft, delicate hair. I was kissing her tiny face. Even then, it felt as if she were saying: "Daddy, this is not good." I then remembered that this is a trial, so I started repeating these words:

((There is no power nor strength except through Allah))

"I have the power to do good and the strength to avoid evil only through Allah's guidance."

((Indeed, we belong to Allah and indeed, to Him we will return.))

I CALLED MY COLLEAGUE Ibrahim and told him to come immediately. My daughter Sarah has passed away. The women in the women's quarters are giving Sarah a bath with my wife. Finally, they finished her bathing.

Then they wrapped her innocent and pure body in a white cloth (shroud). My wife called me and asked me to come inside. I went in to bid farewell to Sarah one last time. I was so exhausted with grief that I nearly collapsed. I controlled myself and kissed her forehead. From that moment, I made a vow to remain steadfast in the path of religion until death. I looked at her mother. Her eyes were weary. Her face was pale, and she was shaking her clothes. I said to her:

"Don't grieve. By Allah's grace, Insha'Allah, she will go straight to paradise. We will meet her there. Now prepare yourself for action so she can intercede for us."

Then I recited the verse from Surah At-Tur in which Allah says:

And those who believed and whose descendants followed them in faith—We will join with them their descendants, and We will not deny them [the reward of] anything of their deeds. Every person, for what he has earned, is retained. [At-Tur: 21]

Sarah's mother began to cry, and I also started to cry. We performed her funeral prayer and then proceeded to the cemetery. I was watching her funeral procession, and it felt as if I was looking at the light that had illuminated the paths of my life. We reached the cemetery, which is a very desolate and frightening place.

Upon entering, we headed towards the grave site. I stood by the edge of the grave. I was thinking about how I would bury my daughter here. Sensing my condition, Ibrahim placed his hand on my shoulder and said, "Ahmad! Exercise patience and resolve." I then descended into the grave myself. I thought, "O Ahmad! This is also your final resting place. It could be today or certainly tomorrow. What preparations have you made for this resting place?"

Ibrahim's voice brought me back from the world of thoughts:

"Ahmad! Take the child."

I placed my little daughter, dressed in the white shroud, on my chest. I wished I could bury her in my chest right there. I embraced her and kissed her as much as I could. Then I placed her on her right side in the grave and said:

((In the name of Allah and on the religion of the Messenger of Allah.))

Then I placed bricks in front of the grave and sealed all the gaps properly. I then emerged from the grave. People began to cover the grave with soil while I could not control my tears.

A Penitent's Memoir

An elderly wise man. We used to sit with him. As he aged, his bones weakened, and his eyesight diminished. He would recount the events of his youth. We used to sit with Ka'b bin Malik (may Allah be pleased with him). He would recall his memories related to the event of staying behind from the Battle of Tabuk. The Battle of Tabuk was the last battle in Islamic history in which the Prophet Muhammad (peace be upon him) personally participated.

The Prophet Muhammad (peace be upon him) announced to the Companions (may Allah be pleased with them) to prepare for departure. He wanted people to thoroughly prepare for the campaign against the people of Tabuk. He also collected expenses for the preparation of the army. Eventually, the number of troops in the army reached thirty thousand. All this was happening during a season when the shade of the trees was pleasant and the fruits had ripened and were ready. This battle was fought in intense heat, over a long distance, against a powerful and stubborn enemy, with a significant number of Muslims.

Their names were not recorded in any register.

According to a hadith reported in Sahih Bukhari and Muslim, Sayyidna Ka'b (may Allah be pleased with him) said:

I was quite wealthy. I had prepared two mounts. I thought that I was more capable of jihad than others. At that very time, I was also seeing the cool, sweet, and pleasant shades and the ripe fruits. I was in this state when the Prophet Muhammad (peace be upon him) set out one morning. I thought to myself:

Tomorrow I will go to the market, buy the necessary supplies, and join the Prophet Muhammad (peace be upon him) and his army. The next day I went to the market, but some items were not available, so I returned.

Then I resolved that, God willing, I would go to the market again the next day, buy the necessary items, and join the Islamic army. The next day, some items were still not available. I firmly decided that, God willing, I would come the following day and obtain the required supplies to join the troops. I kept doing this, and several days passed. I missed the honor of accompanying the Prophet Muhammad (peace be upon him). I would pass through the markets and roam the city, but I did not see anyone except those marked by hypocrisy, or the blind, or the lame, who were considered excused by Allah.

Yes! Sayyidna Ka'b (may Allah be pleased with him) remained behind in the city, while the Prophet Muhammad (peace be upon him) had departed with his thirty thousand companions. When the Prophet Muhammad (peace be upon him) arrived in Tabuk, he surveyed the faces of his devoted companions. When he did not see Ka'b (may Allah be pleased with him), who had participated in the Pledge of Aqabah, he said:

"What has Ka'b bin Malik (may Allah be pleased with him) done?"

A man responded:

"O Messenger of Allah (peace be upon him)! His wealth, luxury, and pride have kept him behind."

Sayyidna Mu'adh bin Jabal (may Allah be pleased with him) immediately said (to that man):

"You have spoken very badly. O Messenger of Allah (peace be upon him)! We see nothing in him but good."

The Prophet Muhammad (peace be upon him) remained silent.

Sayyidna Ka'b (may Allah be pleased with him) said:

When the Prophet Muhammad (peace be upon him) completed the campaign of Tabuk and was returning to Madinah, I began to think about how I could escape his displeasure.

In this regard, I sought help from every reasonable person among my family. By the time the Prophet Muhammad (peace be upon him) entered Madinah with his companions, he first went to the Prophet's Mosque and prayed two units of prayer. Then he appeared before the people.

Then the people who had remained behind came. Each person presented his own excuse and compulsion. Everyone was swearing oaths to prove his honesty. The number of those who had stayed behind was just over eighty. The Prophet Muhammad (peace be upon him) accepted their outward excuses and apologies. He prayed for their forgiveness and left their inner secrets to Allah.

When Sayyidna Ka'b bin Malik (may Allah be pleased with him) came forward and greeted the Prophet Muhammad (peace be upon him), the Prophet Muhammad (peace be upon him) looked at him, then smiled in a way that showed both displeasure and anger, and said:

"Come here."

Sayyidna Ka'b (may Allah be pleased with him) approached and sat down before the Prophet Muhammad (peace be upon him).

The Prophet Muhammad (peace be upon him) asked:

"What held you back? Did you not have a riding camel?"

He replied: "Yes."

The Prophet Muhammad (peace be upon him) said:

"Then what prevented you from coming?"

Sayyidna Ka'b (may Allah be pleased with him) said:

"O Messenger of Allah (peace be upon him)! By Allah, if I were sitting with anyone else from the people of the world, you would see how I would have used excuses to calm his anger. For I have been given the skill to speak and persuade others. But by Allah, I know well that if I were to lie to you today to make you pleased, Allah would soon make you angry with me for another reason. However, if I speak the truth, even though you may be displeased with me, I hope that Allah will forgive me.

O Messenger of Allah (peace be upon him)! I swear by Allah, I had no valid excuse. By Allah, when I stayed behind from you, I was in a state of strength and comfort that I had never experienced before." Saying this, Sayyidna Ka'b (may Allah be pleased with him) fell silent.

The Prophet Muhammad (peace be upon him) turned to the Companions (may Allah be pleased with them) and said:

"He has spoken the truth. Now you should get up and leave, and see when Allah will make a decision regarding you."

Sayyidna Ka'b (may Allah be pleased with him) got up and, dragging his feet, left the mosque in a state of extreme sorrow and distress. He had no idea what decision Allah would make regarding him.

When people saw him leaving in that state, some of them followed him and began reproaching him, saying:

"By Allah, we do not think that you have ever committed a sin before this. You are a poet. Were you unable to come up with excuses and justifications like the other people who stayed behind and offered excuses? Could you not present any excuse that would have made the Prophet Muhammad (peace be upon him) pleased with you? Then you could have sought forgiveness from Allah, and Allah would have forgiven you."

Sayyidna Ka'b (may Allah be pleased with him) said:

"My people continuously reproached me until I decided to retract my previous statement and offer some excuse."

I asked:

"Has anyone else had a similar experience?"

The people said:

"Yes, there are two others who gave the same response as you. They were also sent back with the same message that you were sent back with."

I asked: "Who are those two?"

The people replied: "One of them is Sayyidna Murarah bin Rabi' (may Allah be pleased with him), and the other is Sayyidna Hilal bin Umayyah (may Allah be pleased with him). They are both among those who participated in the Battle of Badr. I found them to be the best examples for me. Now I have firmly resolved, by Allah, that I will not retract my previous statement in the presence of the Prophet Muhammad (peace be upon him) nor will I prove myself to be a liar."

Sayyidna Ka'b (may Allah be pleased with him) then sat in his house in a state of profound sorrow and broken-heartedness. It was not long before the Prophet Muhammad (peace be upon him) forbade people from speaking to Sayyidna Ka'b (may Allah be pleased with him) and his two other companions.

Sayyidna Ka'b (may Allah be pleased with him) narrates that people began to distance themselves from us. They started to behave coldly towards us. I would go to the market, but no one was willing to speak to me. People became completely distant from us, to the extent that they were not the same people we once knew. The walls and streets of the city also seemed to appear distant from us. Even the walls were no longer what we recognized. The earth seemed to be estranged from us and was no longer as we knew it.

My two companions remained at home, weeping continuously, day and night, and did not leave their homes. They worshipped as if they were monks in a monastery. But I would mingle with people, engage in conversation, and sit with them. I would go out, pray in congregation with the people, and walk through the markets. However, no one spoke to me. I would come to the mosque, enter the mosque, present myself to the Prophet Muhammad (peace be upon him), and greet him. I would internally wonder whether he had even moved his blessed lips in response to my greeting.

So, I would pray near the Prophet Muhammad (peace be upon him) and sneak glances at him. When I started to pray, he would turn his attention towards me. And when I focused my attention towards him, he would turn his blessed face away from me.

Sayyidna Ka'b (may Allah be pleased with him) spent several days in that state. His anguish and pain increased daily. He was a highly respected person in his tribe, indeed a highly eloquent and articulate poet. Even great kings and rulers knew him. The fame of his poetry was widespread among prominent people. They longed to meet him. Yet, his situation was that in his own city of Medina, among his own people, no one spoke to him. No one was even willing to look at him. As the estrangement intensified and his hardship and suffering became overwhelming, he was faced with another trial.

One day, while he was wandering in the market, a Christian arrived from the evening and called out:

"Who can take me to Ka'b bin Malik?" People began to point towards Sayyidna Ka'b (may Allah be pleased with him). The Christian approached him and presented a letter from the King of Ghassan. How strange! From the King of Ghassan! The news of his situation had reached the lands of Sham, and the king of the Ghassanids had shown special interest in his matter. What did this king want? To find out, Sayyidna Ka'b (may Allah be pleased with him) opened the letter. It read:

"After praising and glorifying Allah and the salutations, O Ka'b! I have been informed that your companion (the Prophet, peace be upon him) has wronged you and distanced you from his proximity. You do not deserve humiliation and disgrace. Come to us, and we will console and comfort you."

When Sayyidna Ka'b (may Allah be pleased with him) had read the entire letter, he spontaneously said: "Indeed, to Allah we belong and to Him we shall return."

The disbelievers are setting their sights on me. This is also a test. It is a trial and a purely satanic attack. He immediately got up, threw the letter into the oven, and burned it to ashes.

Sayyidna Ka'b (may Allah be pleased with him) did not give any attention to the king's enticement for even a moment. Yes, the paths to the courts of kings had opened before him. The palaces of great and eminent people were now accessible. They were ready to honor and make him their special companion. Yet his own city of Medina was harsh towards him, and people were displeased with him. When he greeted people, no one would respond to his greeting. When he asked someone a question, he received no answer. Despite all this, he remained utterly uninterested in the disbelievers. The accursed Satan was unable to make him falter in his steadfastness or enslave him to the desires of the self. Instead, he threw the letter from the Ghassanid king into the fire and reduced it to ashes.

The cycle of night and day continued, and the days went by. A whole month had passed, and Sayyidna Ka'b (may Allah be pleased with him) was still in that state of distress and calamity. The boycott against him was becoming increasingly severe. The burden of hardship was growing daily. The Messenger of Allah (peace be upon him) did not take any action, and there was no decision from Allah through revelation. When forty days in this state were completed, a messenger from the Prophet (peace be upon him) came to Sayyidna Ka'b (may Allah be pleased with him) and knocked on his door.

Sayyidna Ka'b (may Allah be pleased with him) went outside. He hoped that perhaps the time for easing his difficulties and the alleviation of his hardship had arrived. The messenger of the Prophet (peace be upon him) conveyed this message:

"The Messenger of Allah (peace be upon him) commands you to separate from your wife."

He asked:

"Should I divorce her or what should I do?"

The messenger replied:

"No; do not divorce her, but separate from her and do not come near her."

Sayyidna Ka'b (may Allah be pleased with him) went to his wife and said: "Go to your parents' house and stay there until Allah decides about me." The same message was sent by the Prophet (peace be upon him) to the other two companions of Sayyidna Ka'b (may Allah be pleased with him). Among them, the wife of Sayyidna Hilal bin Umayyah (may Allah be pleased with him) came to the Prophet (peace be upon him) and said: "O Messenger of Allah (peace be upon him)! Hilal bin Umayyah (may Allah be pleased with him) is very old and weak. Can I be permitted to serve him on his behalf?"

The Prophet (peace be upon him) replied:

"Yes, but he should not come near you."

She said: "O Messenger of Allah (peace be upon him)! There is no form of desire or movement in this. He is in extreme grief and distress, and since this matter has arisen, he has been crying day and night."

These days were very heavy on Sayyidna Ka'b (may Allah be pleased with him), and the cruelty against him had become severe. So much so that he began to scrutinize his faith. He would talk to Muslims, but no one would respond to him. He would greet the Messenger of Allah (peace be upon him), but the Prophet (peace be upon him) would not respond to his greeting either. He began to wonder where to go and whom to consult.

Sayyidna Ka'b (may Allah be pleased with him) says:

"When this state of distress and calamity prolonged, I eventually went to Sayyidna Abu Qatadah (may Allah be pleased with him), who was my cousin and dearer to me than anyone else. He was in his garden, and he had closed the door of the garden wall from the inside. I climbed over the wall and entered his garden. I greeted him, but by Allah, he did not even respond to my greeting."

I said to him:

"Abu Qatadah (may Allah be pleased with him)! I ask you by Allah, do you not know that I love Allah and His Messenger (peace be upon him)?" But he remained silent. I repeated my question: "O Abu Qatadah (may Allah be pleased with him), do you acknowledge that I love Allah and His Messenger (peace be upon him)?" But he remained silent again. Then I asked for the third time: "O Abu Qatadah (may Allah be pleased with him), I swear by Allah, do you not know that I love Allah and His Messenger (peace be upon him)?" He then spoke, but only said:

"Allah and His Messenger (peace be upon him) know best."

Sayyidna Ka'b (may Allah be pleased with him) heard this response from his cousin and the person he loved most in the world. They did not know whether he was a believer or not. Hearing this, Sayyidna Ka'b (may Allah be pleased with him) could not control his grief, and tears began to flow from his eyes. He then jumped over the garden wall, went outside, and headed straight to his home. He looked at the walls of the empty house. His wife was not there to sit with him and share his grief, nor was there anyone close to comfort him. It had been fifty days since the Prophet (peace be upon him) had instructed people to cease communication with him. On the first third of the fiftieth night, the verses announcing the acceptance of his repentance were revealed to the Prophet (peace be upon him). Ummul Mu'mineen Sayyidah Umm Salamah (may Allah be pleased with her) said: "O Messenger of Allah (peace be upon him), should we not give the good news of the acceptance of repentance to Sayyidna Ka'b bin Malik (may Allah be pleased with him)?"

The Prophet (peace be upon him) replied:

"If you do, people will flock to him and not let him sleep the entire night."

When the Prophet (peace be upon him) performed the Fajr prayer, he gave the good news of the acceptance of repentance for the three individuals. People started going to them to congratulate them. Sayyidna Ka'b (may Allah be pleased with him) says:

"I performed the Fajr prayer on the roof of my house, and after completing the prayer, I sat in that state of hardship described by Allah, feeling as if I was overwhelmed and the world, despite its vastness, had become narrow for me.

There was nothing more distressing for me than the thought that if I died, the Prophet (peace be upon him) would not lead my funeral prayer, or if he passed away, people would regard me with the same state, that no one would speak to me or perform my funeral prayer. I was lost in this torment when someone stood on the peak of Mount Sila and shouted loudly:

"O Ka'b bin Malik (may Allah be pleased with him), receive the good news!"

Upon hearing this, I immediately prostrated and realized that relief had come from Allah. A man was riding a horse, rushing towards me. Another had shouted from the mountain top. But his voice was louder than the horse. When the man reached me, whom I had heard from the mountain, and he gave me the good news of the acceptance of repentance, I took off both of my garments (tunic and shirt) and gave them to him, as he was the first to bring me the good news of the acceptance of repentance.

By Allah, at that time I had nothing except those two garments, so I borrowed two garments for myself. I then set out to present myself to the Messenger of Allah (peace be upon him), and on the way, people came to me in droves. They congratulated me on the acceptance of repentance and said:

"Congratulations on your repentance being accepted by Allah."

This continued along the way until I entered the mosque. The Prophet (peace be upon him) had a radiant face. When he was happy, his face would shine brightly, as if it were a piece of the moon.

He addressed me and said:

"Today is a blessed day for you. From the day your mother gave birth to you until today, you have never had a day like this."

I asked: "O Messenger of Allah (peace be upon him), is this good news from you alone, or is it from Allah?"

The Prophet (peace be upon him) replied:

"Rather, it is from Allah."

Then he recited the verses related to our acceptance of repentance.

When I sat in front of him, I said: "O Messenger of Allah (peace be upon him)! As part of my repentance, I would like to give all of my wealth in charity for Allah and His Messenger (peace be upon him)." Upon hearing this, the Prophet (peace be upon him) said:

"Do so. However, keep some of your wealth for yourself; it is better for you."

I said:

"O Messenger of Allah (peace be upon him)! Allah has saved me because of my truthfulness. Therefore, I consider it a part of my repentance and vow that as long as I live, I will never abandon the principles of truth and sincerity."

Indeed, Allah accepted the repentance of Sayyidna Ka'b (may Allah be pleased with him) and his two companions, and revealed these verses of the Qur'an which will be recited till the end of time. In Surah At-Tawbah, Allah says:

"And [He also turned] to the three who were left behind until, when the earth was closed in on them despite its vastness, and their souls were constricted within them, and they were certain that there was no fleeing from Allah except to Him, then He forgave them (accepted their repentance), that they might repent. Indeed, Allah is the Accepting of Repentance, the Most Merciful." [Surah At-Tawbah: 118-119]

(Sahih al-Bukhari with Fath: 8/113, Hadith: 4418, Book of the Battles)

In the belly of the fish

Everyone remembers Allah in times of difficulty, but most only remember Him and don't obey and follow Him. And as soon as the hardship is removed, they forget Him and begin to disobey and defy Him. And there are some who remain steadfast in goodness and repentance. Prophet Yunus (peace be upon him) invited his people to embrace faith, but they turned away and showed arrogance and pride. He became angry with them and left the town, boarding a ship to go somewhere else.

When the ship became heavy and the people feared that everyone might drown, they decided that in order to lighten the load of the ship, it was necessary to throw at least one person into the sea. To choose this person, they repeatedly cast lots, but the lot always fell on Prophet Yunus (peace be upon him). Finally, they threw him into the sea. A giant fish (whale) came and swallowed Prophet Yunus (peace be upon him) in a complete and intact state and descended into the depths of the sea.

All this happened extremely quickly. Now Prophet Yunus (peace be upon him) was lost in the darkness. He tried to listen to what was around him and heard that the pebbles lying at the bottom of the sea were glorifying Allah. Allah's said about him in the Quran:

"Finally, he cried out from the darkness: 'O Allah! There is no deity except You; You are pure; indeed, I have been among the wrongdoers.'"

These words of his knocked on the doors of the heavens; knocking them, he received deliverance from Allah. This is the story of Prophet Yunus (peace be upon him).

A contemporary lesson

A contemporary person who describes his own story says:

I was young and had come to believe that life was all about immense wealth, soft and warm beds, and splendid cars. It was a Friday. I was sitting on the beach with my like-minded companions. As usual, all the companions were heedless. I heard the words of the muezzin: "HAYYA 'ALA AS-SALAH" (Come to prayer) and "HAYYA 'ALA AL-FALAH" (Come to success).

I swear that I used to hear the call to prayer all my life. But not a single day did I understand the meaning and concept of success and prosperity. My heart was sealed. And the situation had reached a point where the words of the call to prayer were to me as if they were in a language I did not understand. People around us would spread their carpets and prayer mats and gather for prayer. Meanwhile, at that very time, we were completely oblivious to them, adjusting our swimming gear and air tubes so that we could dive into the depths of the water.

One day, we put on our swimming attire and entered the sea. Gradually, we moved quite far from the shore, until we reached the middle of the deep sea. Everything was in its place, and our sea excursion was proceeding beautifully.

We were at the peak of our enjoyment when suddenly the rubber piece that every swimmer holds between their teeth and lips, to prevent water from entering the mouth and to provide fresh air through the tubes, burst. The piece burst just as air was going into my lungs. Suddenly, the salty water of the sea blocked my airway, and I began to die.

My lungs began to cry out for help. They needed air, whatever kind of air it might be. I was overwhelmed with anxiety and distress, the sea was dark, and my companions were very far from me. I began to sense the gravity of the situation. I was going to die. I started gasping, choking, screaming, and flailing, and I began to feel nauseous from the salty, briny water. Now, in front of my eyes, the tape of my life started playing, and with the very first gasp, I realized how weak and frail I was!

Allah had inflicted a few drops of salty water upon me to show me how powerful and mighty He is. I had now firmly believed that there was no refuge or shelter except Allah. I began to move rapidly and kick my arms and legs to get out of the water. But I was in very deep water. Now the difficulty was not that I was going to die. The real difficulty was what face would I show my Lord? When He asks me about my deeds and character, what will I answer?

The first thing I will be questioned about is prayer, and I have squandered it. I recalled the testimony of monotheism and prophethood and hoped that my end would be upon this declaration of faith. When I said "ASHHADU" (I bear witness), something got stuck in my throat. There was some hidden force and unseen hand that was squeezing my neck and throat to prevent me from uttering this phrase. I tried with all my might. But my tongue could not go beyond "ASHHADU... ASHHADU..."

My heart began to cry out:

"O my Lord! Return me. Just for a moment, for a minute, even for a second." But where?

The fulfillment of this wish was a very distant matter; my awareness and consciousness began to fade away. I was trapped in strange darkness. I only remember up to this point of the incident.

But the scope of my Lord's mercy is very vast. Suddenly, the air began to reach my chest again. The darkness lifted. My eyes opened. I saw that one of my companions was holding the air tube to my mouth and trying to bring me back to consciousness. We were still in the depths of the sea. When I saw the smile on my companion's lips, I understood that I was safe. Now my heart and tongue, and every part of my body cried out:

"I bear witness that there is no deity but Allah. And I bear witness that Muhammad is the Messenger of Allah. Praise be to Allah."

I emerged from the water. My state was completely transformed. I came out as a different person, and my perspective on life changed. Now every day and night began to bring me closer to Allah. I realized the mystery of my existence and the purpose of creation in this world, and I remembered Allah's command:

"And I did not create the jinn and mankind except to worship Me."

It is true that He did not create us in vain. Days continued to pass. I kept remembering this incident.

Then once again I went to the sea, put on my swimming and diving gear, and jumped into the water alone, reaching those same depths of the sea. There, I prostrated before my Lord in a way that I had never prostrated in my life. I prostrated in a place where, according to my strong belief, no human had ever prostrated before Allah. Perhaps on the Day of Judgment that place will bear witness for me, and in return for my prostration in the depths of the sea, Allah may have mercy on me and admit me into His paradise. O Allah, Ameen.

Countless Sins and Boundless Forgiveness

Our Lord is more compassionate and merciful to us than our own mothers and fathers. His mercy can be gauged from the fact that He has kept the door of repentance open for everyone. No matter how much disbelief or polytheism someone has committed, no matter how immersed they have been in rebellion and arrogance, the sea of mercy is still surging for them, and the door of repentance remains open for them. Look at the elderly man whose back had stooped due to old age, whose bones had become weak. He came to the Prophet Muhammad (peace be upon him) while the Prophet (peace be upon him) was sitting with his companions (may Allah be pleased with them), and he was dragging his feet on the ground.

His eyebrows had fallen over his eyes. He came leaning on his walking stick, walking slowly. He stood before the Prophet (peace be upon him) and with a heart-wrenching and sorrowful voice said: "O Messenger of Allah (peace be upon him), what do you say about a person who has committed every kind of sin and has not left out a single one? He has not refrained from any minor or major sin. And if his sins were distributed among all the people on the earth, they would all be drowned. Is there any chance for repentance for such a person?"

The Prophet Muhammad (peace be upon him) looked at him and saw an old man whose back was bent, whose breaths were labored, and who had been broken by the passage of time. After indulging in desires and following pleasures, afflictions and hardships had destroyed him. The Prophet Muhammad (peace be upon him) asked him: "Have you embraced Islam?" He replied: "I bear witness that there is no deity but Allah and I bear witness that you are the Messenger of Allah."

The Prophet Muhammad (peace be upon him) then said: "Perform good deeds and abandon evils, and Allah will turn all your previous sins into good deeds for you."

The elderly man asked: "Will my deceitful acts and wrongdoings also be forgiven?" The Prophet Muhammad (peace be upon him) said: "Yes."

The old man began to loudly proclaim Takbir: "Allahu Akbar. Allahu Akbar. Allahu Akbar." He continued to shout Takbir loudly until he disappeared from the sight of the people.

(Al-Mu'jam Al-Kabir: 7/314, Sahih Al-Targhib wa Al-Tarhib: 3/126, Imam Al-Mundziri stated that the chain of this narration is strong, and Hafiz Ibn Hajar said that it meets the condition of Sahih al-Bukhari.)

Could a Mother Throw Her Child into Fire?

Allah Almighty is more compassionate and merciful to His servants than their own mothers and fathers. In Sahih Bukhari and Sahih Muslim, it is mentioned that after the battle of Hawazin, the Prophet Muhammad (peace be upon him) was presented with the children and women of the disbelieving Hawazin tribe. They were gathered together in one place. When the Prophet (peace be upon him) turned his attention to them, he saw a woman among the captives whose child had gone missing. She was walking with her feet dragging, searching for her child, her heart's delight, her offspring. She was in a state of extreme distress. The intensity of her sorrow had made her lose her senses.

She passed by women with infants and fixed her gaze on the faces of the children, searching for her own child. She wished that she could find her child to hold him to her chest, kiss him, and love him, even if it meant risking her own life. In that state of fervent longing, she found her child. The moment she saw him, her tears dried up, and her senses returned. She rushed to him, embraced him to her chest, and, feeling deep pity for his hunger, thirst, cries, and fatigue, she kissed him and held him tightly.

The compassionate and merciful final Prophet Muhammad (peace be upon him), observed this woman who was exhausted, her fatigue apparent, and saw her intense yearning for her lost child. The child was also distressed, and the mother was deeply sorrowful. The Prophet (peace be upon him) then turned to his companions and asked:

"Do you think this woman would throw her child into the fire?" Meaning, if we were to light a fire and command this woman to throw her child into the flames, would she be willing to do so?

The companions were astonished and said:

"How could she throw her child into the fire, when he is her beloved, a part of her heart, and her own blood? How could she agree to throw him into the fire when she is not even removing him from her chest, continuing to kiss him and wash his face with her tears? How could she ever be willing to throw him into the fire, when she is such a compassionate and merciful mother?"

The companions clearly said:

"No, by Allah! O Messenger of Allah (peace be upon him), she would never be prepared to throw her child into the fire." The Prophet (peace be upon him) then said:

"By Allah! Allah is more merciful to His servants than this mother is to her child."

(Sahih Bukhari, Hadith No. 5356; Sahih Muslim, Hadith No. 2754)

A Few Moments in the Hospital

1. I went to visit a patient and inquire about his well-being in the hospital. When I arrived, I saw that he was a forty-year-old man. His face was fresher than that of anyone else, and he had a very handsome physique. But now his entire body had become paralyzed. No part of his body moved except for slight movements of his head and neck. If someone were to take an axe and chop his body into pieces from his feet to his chest, he would not feel any pain.

He also does not realize when he passes stool or urine, except that the smell indicates it. He is dressed in adult diapers like a child, which the hospital staff changes daily.

When I entered his room, I heard the telephone ringing. He shouted loudly:

"Maulana Sahib! Pick up the receiver before the phone is disconnected."

I picked up the receiver and brought it close to his ear, placing a pillow nearby to support it.

I waited for a while until he had received the call, and then he said:

"Sheikh Sahib! Put the receiver back on the phone."

I returned the receiver to its place and then asked him: "How long have you been in this condition?" He replied: "Twenty years. And I have been bedridden like this ever since."

2. Some of my learned companions told me that while passing by a hospital room, they heard a patient shouting loudly. His cries were so

heart-wrenching and agonizing that they were shattering the heart and liver. My learned friend said that when he entered the patient's room, he saw that the man's entire body was completely paralyzed, and he was trying to turn over but was unsuccessful in his attempt.

I asked the nurse on duty about the reason for his shouting, and she explained that his entire body was paralyzed, and his intestines had also been affected. He suffers from indigestion and stomach pain after every meal, both at lunch and dinner.

I advised her:

"Do not give him heavy or rich food. Avoid giving him meat and rice." She replied:

You know what we feed him? By Allah! We do not feed him anything except for delivering milk to his stomach through a tube inserted into his nose. All these hardships are only for digesting the milk.

3. Another friend of mine told me that I passed by a patient who was paralyzed and whose entire body could not move. He said:

What I see is that the patient was shouting at people passing through the corridor. I entered his room. I saw a wooden lectern in front of him, and the Quran was open on it. This patient had been reciting only two pages for several hours. When he reached the end from the beginning, he started again from the new. His repeating these two pages over and over was merely due to his inability to turn the pages of the Quran and his lack of power and ability to move his hands. There was no one present to help him turn the pages of the Quran.

When I stood in front of him, he addressed me and said:

Please turn the page forward. I turned to the next page of the Quran, and his face brightened. Then he fixed his gaze on the Quran and began reciting. I started crying profusely in front of him. My crying was because of his deep eagerness and desire for recitation and my own carelessness and neglect.

4. A third acquaintance of mine told me an incident that he passed by a hospital where there was a patient who was completely paralyzed and entirely incapacitated, only his head moved. When he saw him in this heartbreaking condition, he felt a lot of sympathy for him and asked:

What is your wish or desire? He thought. He would say that his utmost desire and greatest wish is to recover. To get up. To sit. To lie down. To be able to move around here and there. But this sick and helpless person expressed a different desire.

He said:

I am approximately forty years old and have five children. I have been stuck on this bed for the past seven years. By Allah! My desire is not to walk. Nor is it my wish to see my children, and neither is it a desire to live a normal life like other people.

He was asked:

It is surprising. If you do not wish for any of these things, then what is your desire and wish?

He said:

My utmost desire is only to have enough ability to place my forehead in prostration before Allah and to be able to perform prostration in the same way as other people do.

5. This incident was narrated to me by a doctor who, when entering the intensive care unit to see a patient, found an elderly distinguished person lying on a white bed, with radiance playing on his face. My colleague told me that as I flipped through his file, I discovered that

he had undergone surgery. During the operation, there was excessive blood loss, and this resulted in the circulation of blood in some parts of his brain stopping, and he became completely unconscious and unresponsive. An artificial respiratory system was established with medical equipment, and through the artificial breathing apparatus placed on his mouth, nine breaths per minute were being delivered to his lungs. His son was standing nearby. When I asked him about his father, he said that his father had been serving as a muezzin in a mosque for several years. I started looking at the patient, I shook his hand, moved his eye, and tried to talk to him. But he was not aware of anything. His condition was extremely critical. His son began talking close to his ear, although he was unable to understand anything.

The boy began to speak:

Father! "Mother" is well and safe, all the siblings are also fine, and uncle has returned safely from his journey.

The boy kept talking, and the patient remained in his original condition. There was no movement in his body. The artificial respiration apparatus continued delivering air to his lungs at nine breaths per minute.

Suddenly, the son began to say:

The mosque is sad without you and eager to see you. Only so-and-so person calls the adhan, and he makes mistakes in the adhan. The mosque has an empty place where you used to stand. As the son started talking about the mosque and the adhan, the respected Shaykh's heart began to beat, and he started breathing. At that very moment, I looked at the artificial respiration machine, and its meter was showing eighteen breaths per minute. But the boy was unaware of this.

Then the boy began to speak again:

Our cousin has gotten married. Our brother has completed his education. The Shaykh's breathing became faint again, and the machine started showing nine breaths per minute. When I saw this scene, I moved closer to the Shaykh, stood by his bedside, and shook his hand. He opened his eyes and looked around. I moved him, but nothing happened. Everything was still in its place; he did not respond to my shaking. I was greatly astonished.

I placed my mouth close to his ear and said in a long tone (like the adhan):

"Allah is the Greatest. Come to the prayer, come to success."

While saying this, I also watched the artificial respiration machine. It began showing eighteen breaths per minute again. Such qualities in patients are from Allah alone. By Allah, it is not they who are patients, but we are the patients. What kind of patients are those whose hearts are attached to the mosques? Yes! Allah Almighty has spoken about such people:

"Men whom neither trade nor sale distracts from the remembrance of Allah and the establishment of prayer and the giving of zakah. They fear a Day when hearts and eyes will tremble. That Allah may reward them according to the best of what they did and increase them from His bounty. And Allah gives provision to whom He wills without account." [An-Nur: 37-38]

This is the condition of patients and bedridden sick people. O person safe from diseases and illnesses! Look into your own condition. O person free from all kinds of suffering and pain! O person nurtured in Allah's blessings! Who is not the slightest bit afraid of Allah's wrath and retribution! What has Allah done to you that you are disobeying Him in return? What harm has He inflicted upon you? Have His blessings not been descending upon you one after another? And His grace and kindness towards you are beyond your estimation and calculation. Do you not fear that on the Day of Judgment you will be held accountable before Allah? And Allah will ask:

"My servant, did I not grant you health and safety in your body? Did I not bestow upon you ample and abundant sustenance? Did I not protect your ears and eyes?"

At that time, you will say: "Yes, it was just as you said." Then the Lord of Might and Majesty, the Lord of the worlds, will ask:

"Why did you show ingratitude for My blessings and disobey Me? And why did you become a victim of My wrath and retribution?"

Then, all your flaws will be exposed before the entire universe, and your sins will be presented to you one by one. May these sins be destroyed. How severe is their curse and danger?

- What drowned the people of Noah (peace be upon him) in the flood if not their sins?

- What destroyed the people of 'Aad and Thamud if not their sins?

- The people of Prophet Lot (peace be upon him) had their town overturned and thrown down.

- The people of Prophet Shu'ayb (peace be upon him) were immediately seized by punishment.

- Abraha was pelted with harsh, rocky stones.

- Pharaoh was struck with a deadly punishment.

What was the cause of all these if not disobedience and sins?

Mountains of Faith and Determination

At the beginning of his prophethood, the Prophet Muhammad (peace be upon him) used to invite people to Islam in secret in Mecca, and the Muslims also concealed their faith. When the number of Muslims reached thirty-eight men, Abu Bakr Siddiq (may Allah be pleased with him) insisted that the Prophet Muhammad (peace be upon him) should publicly declare himself and openly invite others to Islam.

The Prophet (peace be upon him) said:

"O Abu Bakr! We are still very few in number."

Abu Bakr Siddiq (may Allah be pleased with him) continued to insist until the Prophet Muhammad (peace be upon him) went out to the Sacred Mosque. The Muslims went out with him and dispersed around the mosque. Each person reached their own family. Abu Bakr Siddiq (may Allah be pleased with him) stood among the people and began to speak. He was the first preacher in the field of inviting to Allah at that time. When the polytheists saw that this man was speaking ill of their deities and pointing out faults in their religion, they all attacked Abu Bakr Siddiq (may Allah be pleased with him) and the other Muslims. They began to beat them severely inside the Sacred Mosque. Abu Bakr (may Allah be pleased with him) continued to openly profess his Islam until a group of polytheists surrounded him and beat him so badly that he fell to the ground.

He was advanced in age, around fifty years old. The wicked and sinful 'Utbah ibn Rabi'ah approached him, climbed on his abdomen and chest, and began to beat him with his double-soled shoes. He rubbed his face with the shoes until he had pierced the flesh of his face. His blood flowed so much that it became difficult to distinguish his nose from his face. He was in a state of fainting. Finally, members of his tribe, Banu Taym, came forward and drove the attacking polytheists away.

People wrapped him in a cloth and carried him away. They were certain that he had died. However, they took him to his house. His father and other tribe members sat by his side, shaking him, but he did not respond. As the day drew to a close and the shadows of the evening grew longer, he regained some consciousness. He opened his eyes, and the first sentence that came from his lips was:

"What is the condition of the Prophet Muhammad (peace be upon him)?"

Upon hearing this, his father, who had not yet embraced Islam, became very angry, rebuked him, and then left. His mother then sat by his side, trying to feed and persuade him. But the only thing he kept repeating was:

"WHAT HAPPENED TO THE Prophet Muhammad (peace be upon him)? What is his condition?"

His mother said:

"By Allah, I have no knowledge about your companion."

He told his mother to go to Umm Jamil bint al-Khattab (may Allah be pleased with her, the sister of Umar ibn al-Khattab) and inquire about the Prophet Muhammad (peace be upon him). Umm Jamil (Fatimah bint Khattab) had embraced Islam but, like others, was still concealing her faith.

Abu Bakr Siddiq's (may Allah be pleased with him) mother left her house and arrived at the house of Umm Jamil (may Allah be pleased with her). She said to her:

"Abu Bakr (may Allah be pleased with him) wants to know about the well-being of Muhammad (peace be upon him)."

Umm Jamil (may Allah be pleased with her) was afraid that this might reveal her own embrace of Islam. She said:

"I do not know Abu Bakr (may Allah be pleased with him), nor do I recognize Muhammad (peace be upon him). But if you wish, I am ready to go with you to see your son."

Abu Bakr Siddiq's (may Allah be pleased with him) mother agreed, and she went with her. When they reached Abu Bakr (may Allah be pleased with him), they saw him severely injured and in a critical state, with his face's flesh torn and blood flowing. Seeing this scene, she began to weep and said:

Your people have beaten you so much that you are in this condition. By Allah! Those people are indeed very sinful and disbelieving. I hope Allah will surely take revenge on them for you. Upon hearing their voices, Sayyidina Abu Bakr (may Allah be pleased with him) turned towards them and said:

"O Umm Jamil (may Allah be pleased with her)! What news of the Messenger of Allah (peace be upon him)?"

Lady Umm Jamil (may Allah be pleased with her) looked at Sayyidina Abu Bakr's (may Allah be pleased with him) mother, who had not yet converted to Islam. She was afraid that she might reveal the Muslims' secrets to the disbelievers, so she addressed Sayyidina Siddiq (may Allah be pleased with him) and said:

"Your mother is listening."

He said:

"Do not be afraid of her presence. She will not cause you any harm."

Lady Umm Jamil (may Allah be pleased with her) then said:

"Allah's Messenger (peace be upon him) is safe and sound and in good health."

Sayyidina Abu Bakr (may Allah be pleased with him) asked:

"Where is the Prophet (peace be upon him)?"

She replied that the Noble Prophet (peace be upon him) was staying at the house of Sayyidina Arqam (may Allah be pleased with him).

Then Sayyidina Abu Bakr's (may Allah be pleased with him) mother said:

"You have learned about your companion (the Prophet, peace be upon him). Now eat and drink something."

He said:

"No, by Allah! I will not eat anything until I personally come to the Prophet (peace be upon him) and see him with my own eyes, safe and sound."

The two women advised him to wait a while. When the darkness of night fell and the people had stopped coming and going in the street, Sayyidina Abu Bakr as-Siddiq (may Allah be pleased with him) tried to get up but could not. His mother and Lady Umm Jamil (may Allah be pleased with her) helped him, and they took him to the Prophet (peace be upon him).

When the Noble Prophet (peace be upon him) saw him in that condition, he bent over him and began to kiss him. All the Muslims present there gathered around him. Seeing him in that state caused the Noble Prophet (peace be upon him) to be deeply moved. Sayyidina Abu Bakr as-Siddiq (may Allah be pleased with him) said with his own tongue:

"O Messenger of Allah (peace be upon him)! My mother and father are sacrificed for you (peace be upon him). I am unharmed. Only the condition of my face, which was caused by that sinful Utbah, is what pains me."

Then Sayyidina Abu Bakr (may Allah be pleased with him) requested:

"O Messenger of Allah (peace be upon him)! This is my mother, and she is very kind and benevolent towards her son. You are a blessed person; invite her to Allah, convey the message of Islam to her, and pray to Allah for her guidance. Perhaps, through you (peace be upon him), Allah might save her from the fire of Hell."

The Noble Prophet (peace be upon him) prayed for her guidance and invited her to Allah and the religion of Islam, and she embraced Islam right there.

(Bidaya wa Nihaya by Ibn Kathir: 3/30)

Look at this strong and great mountain of faith and resolve—Sayyidina Abu Bakr as-Siddiq (may Allah be pleased with him). Reflect on his deep interest in invitation and preaching, and be astounded by his steadfastness and resolve in Islam. Have you ever looked into your own soul and asked yourself:

What service have you rendered to Islam?

How many people have come to the path of guidance as a result of your invitation, preaching, and good conduct?

Have you faced any trials and hardships in the way of Allah?

Do you command good and forbid evil?

Show courage and bravery and play a strong role in this field. Stand firm as mountains of resolve against the difficulties faced in invitation and preaching. Allah will be your supporter and helper and will guide you on the straight path.

I seek refuge in Allah

There was a poor and destitute young man. He would wander the streets, selling items to make a living. There was a wealthy, carefree woman who did not refrain from engaging in illicit activities. She was a trap set by Satan. One day, as the young man passed by her house, she slightly opened the door and peeked outside, asking him: "What are you selling?"

He informed her. The woman asked the young man to come inside as she wanted to see the items. When he entered, she locked the door from inside and invited him to commit adultery and immorality. The young man shouted at her and said:

"Ma'adh Allah! (I seek refuge in Allah)." He then began to remember the time when all pleasures would vanish, and regrets would surround him. He recalled the day when the very body parts that enjoyed the sin would testify against him. The feet with which he walked, the hands with which he touched, the tongue with which he spoke obscenities—indeed, every part of his body would testify against him.

The young man remembered the heat of Hellfire and the punishments from Allah. He recalled the day and the scene when those who committed adultery would be hung in Hell. They would be beaten with iron whips. Whenever someone would cry out in distress from this beating, the angels would say:

"Where was this voice when you laughed out loud? You were joyful and engaged in amusement, without a care for Allah, nor did you feel any modesty before Him?"

The young man remembered the saying of the Prophet Muhammad (peace be upon him) in which he said:

"O nation of Muhammad! By Allah, there is none more protective of his honor than Allah, that His servant or maidservant should commit adultery. O nation of Muhammad! By Allah, if you knew what I know, you would laugh little and weep much." (Sahih Muslim, hadith number 901)

He remembered the day when the Prophet Muhammad (peace be upon him) saw in a dream the men and women who committed adultery, who were naked and confined in a narrow place similar to a bread oven, broad at the bottom and narrow at the top. They were screaming and shouting. Flames of fire would rise from underneath them, and when these flames would rise, the severe heat would cause them to scream.

The Prophet (peace be upon him) asked, "O Jibreel (Gabriel), who are these people?"

He replied, "These are the men and women who committed adultery."

This punishment will continue until the Day of Judgment, and the punishment in the Hereafter will be even more severe and eternal. We pray to Allah for forgiveness, mercy, and safety. The young man was tempted by his evil self, which advised him: "Do it now and repent later."

But he said:

"I seek refuge in Allah. How can I violate the limits set by Allah and tear apart this veil? How can I look at this woman when it is not permissible for me, while Allah is watching us from above? How can we remain hidden from the creation when we commit such sinful acts in front of the Creator?"

He thought silently for a while about how to escape this situation. His eyes were fixed on the door. Meanwhile, the sinful woman threatened him, saying that if he did not do what she wanted, she would scream and gather the people around, accusing him of trying to violate her honor. She said his end would be either death or imprisonment at the very least.

The virtuous young man laughed at this situation.

He tried to instill the fear of Allah in the wicked woman, but she did not relent. Seeing all this, he started thinking of a way to escape from her. Finally, he said he wanted to go to the toilet. The woman pointed towards it.

When he entered the toilet, he looked at the windows and realized that he couldn't escape through them. Now, the only way to free himself was to cover himself in filth. So, he did just that and smeared the toilet filth on his hands, body, and clothes. He then stood before the sinful woman in this state.

When she saw him like this, she screamed and threw the items he was selling at his face and pushed him out of the house. As he walked through the street, children followed him, shouting "crazy, crazy," until he reached his home. He changed his clothes, bathed, and cleaned himself.

From that time on, his body continuously emitted a pleasant fragrance, until he passed away from this transient world to the eternal abode.

They attained Paradise.

———

Ma'iz bin Malik Aslami (may Allah be pleased with him) was a handsome young man from among the Companions. He was already married in Medina. One day, Satan put a whisper in his heart and tempted him regarding a maidservant of an Ansari companion. He took her to a secluded place out of sight of people, and Satan became the third between them, swaying their minds and making them appear beautiful to each other until they committed the sinful act of adultery.

When Ma'iz (may Allah be pleased with him) finished this sinful act, Satan left his mind, and he was overwhelmed with grief and remorse. He began to cry intensely, blaming and accounting for himself. He was so afraid of Allah's punishment that life became unbearable for him. The guilt of his sin started to torment him until it burned his heart to ashes.

He then went to the one who heals hearts, the spiritual doctor, the wise guide of the Ummah, Muhammad the Messenger of Allah (peace be upon him). Standing before him, he said:

"O Messenger of Allah (peace be upon him)! This servant has committed adultery. Purify me by giving me the punishment for this sin."

The Prophet (peace be upon him) turned his blessed face away. Ma'iz moved to stand in front of him again and said:

"O Messenger of Allah (peace be upon him)! I have committed adultery. Purify me by giving me the punishment."

The Prophet (peace be upon him) said:

"May Allah forgive you! Go back and seek repentance and forgiveness from Allah."

He turned back a little but could not bear it, and he returned to the Prophet (peace be upon him) and said:

"O Messenger of Allah (peace be upon him)! Impose the punishment for adultery on me and purify me from this sin."

The Prophet (peace be upon him) admonished him, saying:

"May Allah forgive you! Go back and repent to Allah and seek His forgiveness."

The narrator states that he went back a little but soon returned and started crying:

"O Messenger of Allah (peace be upon him)! Purify me."

The Prophet (peace be upon him) then, in a loud and stern voice, said:

"May you be ruined! Do you even know what adultery is?" Then the Prophet (peace be upon him) ordered that he be taken away from in front of him. However, Ma'iz kept returning repeatedly. When his persistence increased, the Prophet (peace be upon him) asked his family and tribe:

"Is this young man insane?"

The people replied:

"O Messenger of Allah (peace be upon him)! We have not seen any signs of illness in him."

The Prophet (peace be upon him) then said:

"Perhaps he is drunk and saying all this under the influence of alcohol?"

A man stood up and went near Ma'iz to smell his breath, but found no smell of alcohol.

Then the Prophet (peace be upon him) asked:

"Do you know what adultery is?"

He replied:

"Yes! I have committed a sinful act with a woman and did with her what a man lawfully does with his wife."

The Prophet (peace be upon him) asked:

"What do you intend to say by this?"

He replied that he wanted the Prophet (peace be upon him) to impose the legal punishment on him and purify him from this sin.

The Prophet (peace be upon him) then said:

"Alright." And he ordered his Companions (may Allah be pleased with them) to stone the young man. Consequently, he was stoned to death as a result of which he passed away.

After his funeral prayer was offered and he was buried, the Prophet (peace be upon him) and some of his Companions (may Allah be pleased with them) passed by the place where he was stoned. The Prophet (peace be upon him) overheard two men talking. One said to the other:

"Look at this man. Allah had concealed his sin, but he did not keep it hidden, and he was stoned to death like a dog."

The Prophet (peace be upon him) remained silent upon hearing this and walked on for a while. Then he came across the carcass of a dead donkey, swollen from the heat of the sun with its legs sticking upwards.

When the Prophet (peace be upon him) saw the dead donkey, he said:

"Where are those two men?"

They said:

"O Messenger of Allah (peace be upon him)! We are here."

The Prophet (peace be upon him) said:

"Dismount and eat the flesh of this dead donkey."

They replied:

"O Prophet of Allah (peace be upon him)! Who would eat the flesh of a dead donkey?"

The Prophet (peace be upon him) said:

"The sin you have committed by backbiting your stoned brother is worse than eating the flesh of this putrid carcass. This young man has repented in such a way that if his repentance were to be distributed among the entire Ummah, it would be sufficient for all of them. By the One in whose hand is my soul! That young man is now enjoying the pleasures of Paradise and is diving into its rivers."

How fortunate is Sayyiduna Ma'iz bin Malik (may Allah be pleased with him)! Yes, he committed the sin of adultery. He tore the veil between himself and his Lord, but then he repented in such a manner that if his repentance were to be distributed among the entire Ummah, it would suffice to forgive all their sins.

[This incident is found in both Sahih Bukhari (4970) and Sahih Muslim (1691), and we have presented the essence of its various narrations.]

A Singer's Repentance

He said while holding back his tears:

She was standing by the window, looking at me with tear-filled eyes and gesturing with those hands that had been weakened and emaciated by the passage of time. She was trying to hold back her tears, but she was overwhelmed by emotions of lamentation and began to weep uncontrollably.

I stopped and started looking at her. The sound of her crying reached my ears, but a thick and heavy layer of my sins was sitting on my chest, obstructing the path of her lamentations from reaching my stone-hard heart.

I rejected all her pleas to stay with her and did not give even a straw's worth of importance to her advice and counsel to enroll in a university in our own city and complete my education. The quest for selfishness, egotism, fake and hollow freedom, and the dreams of an independent personality, rather the enslavement to desires and lusts, the captivity of sensual pleasures, and the siege of all the devils of humans and jinn had united to mislead me.

I fled from her advice and counsel. I ran away from her affection and love-filled motherhood. But she was afraid that I might fall into moral deviation and waywardness. I left her standing at the window saying goodbye. I disappeared from her sight, but she remained standing there.

In my heart, I said: Goodbye, mother!

A long time passed while I was absent from my mother. When I left the house, I did not even get to hear these words: Son! I entrust you to Allah. Son! Where are you going? There, I did not get to hear these words: Son! Why are you so late?

I became engrossed in a life of play and amusement, a life in which there was nothing but negligence and disobedience and sin.

"My voice is very melodious."

Saying this, my bad companions started presenting singing in front of me in an adorned manner, and I started singing. The devils in human forms hovering around me began showering me with praises. Their applause created a soft spot in my heart.

Finally, the day came when I was formally invited to sing on stage. Now, I fell into a strange turmoil and a terrifying conflict about what to do. A sense of modesty and shame still occupied a small space in my heart. For a while, I remained in a mixed state of yes and no.

My heart was reproaching me. Never. I will not stand on stage and sing like those immoral people. But at the same time, my devilish self was rebuking and cursing me. This is a golden opportunity for you. Don't let it slip away. You will become a famous artist. After much hesitation and reluctance, I finally accepted the invitation.

I climbed the stage, but there were still a few drops of modesty left in my heart. However, with the first words of the song, the remaining modesty disappeared. The entire hall echoed with music. People were swaying and enjoying themselves. Whenever I paused, the applause and praise of the people encouraged me to keep singing. That night passed, but it ended the remaining faith I had.

The number of my bad friends began to increase. Invitations to perform became frequent. I began to rush from one stage to another. Various sins and different acts of disobedience began. There were general all-night gatherings and special night programs. I was invited to participate in a major music and singing program at a palace. I performed some songs that the audience enjoyed immensely. I was indeed a rising and shining new star in the world of singing and music. After the music festival or celebration, I received an invitation from a great artist who offered to train me and take me under his wing to refine my talent.

Through his manager, I secured an appointment with this famous artist to arrange the details. Thursday was set for the appointment. Days and nights passed quickly. Two days before the set date, I came home to attend some family events. The house was filled with continuous joy and excitement. My brother's wedding was on Thursday, and my two sisters' engagement ceremonies were scheduled for Wednesday.

My mother was jubilant, buzzing like a honeybee here and there, overflowing with joy. She was responding to people's blessings and congratulations with equal joy. Her lips were so filled with happiness that if distributed, everything in the universe would start smiling. She was busy day and night preparing for the grand wedding ceremony. She wanted to personally ensure every little thing was in order. She was inquiring about every small and big thing.

Thursday arrived very quickly, but on that day, an incident occurred that changed the course of my life. That tragic event woke me from my deep sleep of heedlessness. This calamity revived my dead heart.

This incident pulled me out of the swamp of filth, the mud of humiliation and degradation, and removed me from the dirty pond of singing and music, placing me in a clean place. My mother passed away. How?

I do not know. But the important thing is that she passed away. But before that, she shared in our joy. Then she moved a little aside and laid her tired body on her bed. It was as if she was saying with her state:

"My children! Goodbye. Now you have grown up."

The joyful celebration turned into mourning and sorrow. Every face became sad and silent. A sense of terror spread, and this unexpected tragedy silenced everyone. Every eye was filled with tears, and hearts were trembling. The sound of sobs was rising from every corner of the house. Everything was engaged in weeping and wailing. Except for my mother. She lay peacefully on her bed, unaware of what was happening around her.

The family began to bathe her. When the process of shrouding and burial preparation was completed, I entered the room where her body lay in a white shroud. I had one last look at her. Her face appeared just as peaceful and serene as it did in life.

I looked deeply at her face, her eyes, and her hands. Until yesterday, this mother of mine used to stop me from going away from her out of fear that I might go astray. I kissed her, cried my heart out, and my sisters standing around me also cried their hearts out. Eventually, they took me out of the room where she was being washed and shrouded.

Several moments passed quickly, without me realizing it. Suddenly, I found myself standing in line, praying her funeral prayer. Her body lay motionless, and the Imam was repeating "Allahu Akbar, Allahu Akbar." From the depths of my heart and soul, I prayed for her and also prayed that Allah forgive me for the shortcomings and negligence in serving her.

Along with others, I shouldered her coffin and carried it to her final resting place in the cemetery. I began to pour soil over her grave, and a spontaneous prayer flowed from my tongue:

"O Allah, keep her steadfast. O Allah, grant her firmness."

The entire day was spent among those offering condolences, but the night was a different story.

Tonight, I entered my bedroom a little earlier. I turned off all the lights and let myself collapse onto the bed. Now, the film of the past began to play before my eyes, with each picture vividly appearing on the screen of my mind. My mother's voice echoed in my ears and around me:

"My son! Get up. Don't miss your prayer time. Your friends are waiting for you at the mosque."

Sometimes these voices would strike my eardrums:

"O my dear son! Stay with me, don't leave me, continue your education. Don't embark on this journey."

"Son! Take care of yourself."

Clouds of regret, remorse, sorrow, and worry overshadowed my chest, making it difficult for me to breathe due to their weight on my heart. A reel of disobedience began to play, presenting all those scenes one by one before my eyes.

My mother always strove to bestow blessings and happiness upon me, while I constantly subjected her to grief. She filled my life with joy, while I made her cry. I began to recall each moment when she would plead with hope and beg me not to go out and avoid doing wrong things. Now, I am sighing over them and shedding tears of regret. Oh! How disobedient I was to my mother. What will be my fate in the Hereafter, while the Prophet (peace and blessings of Allah be upon him) said:

"He who severs ties of kinship will not enter Paradise." (Sahih al-Bukhari, No. 5638)

Is there any mercy and relationship greater than that of my mother? I fear that Allah might immediately punish me for this sin, which could manifest as my children's disobedience towards me.

I cried out: O my Lord! Forgive me. If only my mother could return to this world and I could kiss her head and ask for her forgiveness. I would place my head at her feet and wash them with my tears of remorse.

What harm had she done to me to deserve such cold treatment from me? What was her fault that I adopted this arrogant attitude towards her?

Isn't she the one who carried me in her womb for nine months? Then endured the pains of childbirth and spent sleepless nights for my comfort during my childhood?

Ah! How hard my heart is!

My state towards my father was even worse. I cried a lot. I stood up for the funeral prayer but couldn't recite anything. My tongue was tied. My tears were very hot. They melted and softened the hardness of my heart. Now, as I prostrated, I soaked the place of prostration with my tears. A cry was rising from the depths of my heart. Sincere prayers were flowing from my tongue, and every fiber of my being was saying "Ameen, Ameen."

I made a vow to my Lord that I would always pray for forgiveness and mercy for my mother after her death and, to the best of my ability, would not withhold from giving charity on her behalf for her reward.

I also prayed to my Lord, O Allah! Help me to keep this vow and remain steadfast upon it. And I repeatedly prayed:

"O Allah, O Turner of hearts, keep my heart firm upon Your religion."

I completed the funeral prayer. Now, I looked back at my dark and despairing past. When I flipped through the records of my deeds and the pages of my actions, I found a register of some of my songs. A bundle of letters from fans was lying somewhere. There were photo albums made with people and from various programs. A cassette of my famous and popular songs was lying in one place, along with cassettes of songs by other wicked people.

I reached into my pocket and took out all the cards. Among them was a card from a very famous artist. Seeing it, I remembered my appointment with him on Thursday afternoon.

I cried out, "I seek refuge in Allah!"

I tore that card into pieces with my own hands. Now, I gathered everything around me that reminded me of my sins and disobedience. I put them all in a sack. The next day, I got rid of them forever.

The Story of a Great Hero of Islam

———

He was a handsome young man. He was raised and nurtured in a respected, dignified, and powerful family. He was greatly honored and revered in his community and had a formidable presence in his country and region. He was a prominent figure among his peers and a unique person of his time—indeed, a rare gem of his age. This is Sayyidina Salman al-Farsi (may Allah be pleased with him)!

He was a fire-worshipping Magian, who practiced the worship of fire. His father was the chief of his people, and he dearly loved his promising son. He kept him near the fire in their home.

After staying near the fire for a long time, he worked hard to learn Magianism until he became a person who kindled the fire, rather than just worshipped it.

His father had a large garden, and he used to go there daily. One day, while his father was busy with some construction work in their home, he addressed his son and said: "Salman, go to my estate and carry out the tasks I have assigned."

Sayyidina Salman (may Allah be pleased with him) was very pleased. He left the confinement and headed straight to the garden. On his way to the garden, he passed by a Christian monastery. Hearing the sounds of worship from there, he entered the monastery to see what they did. He found their manner of worship and their ritual appealing and desired to follow their practice. He thought to himself that this religion was better than the Magianism and fire-worship he was accustomed to. He asked the Christians about their religion and learned that its center was in Syria, and their greatest scholar was also there.

He remained with them until sunset, and he was delayed in returning to his father.

When he finally returned, his father asked him: "My son, where have you been until now?"

He replied: "I passed by some people who were worshipping in their church. Their way of worship and their rituals were pleasing to me. I also felt that their religion is better than our religion." His father was alarmed and said:

"O my son! Your religion and the religion of your forefathers is far better than their religion."

In response, he immediately said: "By Allah, this cannot be the case. The fact is that their religion is far better than ours."

His father became apprehensive that he might abandon Magianism. Thus, he shackled his feet and imprisoned him in their home. When Sayyidina Salman (may Allah be pleased with him) experienced this treatment from his father, he sent a messenger to the Christians, informing them that he was pleased with their religion and desired to embrace it. He requested them to inform him when a delegation from the Christians of Syria would arrive.

Not long after, a delegation from Syria, consisting of Christian traders, came to him. They sent a messenger with a message, which Sayyidina Salman (may Allah be pleased with him) received. He responded by saying that when the traders concluded their business and planned to return, he should be informed.

When the traders finalized their plans to return, they informed Sayyidina Salman (may Allah be pleased with him) and arranged a meeting place. Sayyidina Salman (may Allah be pleased with him) managed to free himself from the shackles and proceeded from his home to the designated place, then traveled with the traders to Syria. Upon reaching Syria, he inquired about the greatest scholar of Christianity. They replied: "It is the priest who is in the monastery."

Sayyidina Salman (may Allah be pleased with him) went to the monastery and informed the bishop of his entire situation. He told him that he wished to embrace the religion and to stay with him, serve him, worship with him, and learn from him.

The bishop replied: "You may stay with me."

Thus, Sayyidina Salman (may Allah be pleased with him) began living in the monastery with the bishop.

Sayyidina Salman (may Allah be pleased with him) dedicated himself to good deeds, welfare activities, and worship. However, the bishop was the worst person in terms of his Christianity. He ordered people to give charity and encouraged them to do so, but when they collected a large amount of charity, he kept it for himself, sitting on it like a snake and not giving it to the poor and needy. For these and other reasons, Sayyidina Salman (may Allah be pleased with him) developed a strong aversion to him. Yet, he could not say anything about it because the bishop was highly respected among people. Meanwhile, Sayyidina Salman (may Allah be pleased with him) was a stranger and had only recently entered Christianity.

It wasn't long before the bishop died. His people were deeply grieved by his death. Everyone gathered to perform his washing, shrouding, and burial.

He was a stranger and had only recently embraced Christianity.

It wasn't long before the bishop died. His people were very saddened by his death. Everyone gathered to perform his washing, shrouding, and burial.

When Sayyidina Salman (may Allah be pleased with him) saw the sorrow and grief of the people, he said:

"This bishop was not a good man. He was among the evil scholars of Christianity. He commanded you to give charity and encouraged you to do so. But when you brought wealth and collected it for him, he kept it as his personal treasure and did not give anything to the poor and needy."

The people asked: "What evidence do you have for this?"

He replied: "I will show you the location of his treasure."

He took the people to the place where the treasure was hidden. When they dug up the place, they found seven large containers filled with gold and silver.

The people then began to say: "By Allah, we will not bury him." They actually crucified him on a piece of wood.

After that, they brought another person and appointed him as the new bishop in the monastery. Sayyidina Salman (may Allah be pleased with him) reported that he found this new bishop to be very devout. He was detached from the world and sought the Hereafter. His days and nights were spent in worship. Sayyidina Salman (may Allah be pleased with him) loved him so much that he thought he had never loved anyone as much.

Sayyidina Salman (may Allah be pleased with him) continued to serve him until he became very old and eventually death overtook him. Sayyidina Salman (may Allah be pleased with him) was deeply saddened by his departure and feared whether he would be able to remain steadfast in the religion after him.

Before the bishop died, he asked him:

"You see that the divine decree (time of death) has indeed arrived for you. Tell me, whom should I follow now?"

He said:

"My son, by Allah, I do not know anyone who has beliefs and practices like mine. People have altered the religion. They have fallen into destruction and have abandoned many of their beliefs and practices. However, there is a person in the city of Mosul (Iraq) whose beliefs and practices are like mine. He is a person by the name of so-and-so. You should immediately go to him."

When this devout and ascetic man passed away, Sayyidina Salman (may Allah be pleased with him) left Syria and went to Iraq, where he joined this person in Mosul. He stayed with him until that person passed away. But in his last moments, this Christian monk advised Sayyidina Salman (may Allah be pleased with him) to go to a person living in the region of Nisibis (Syria).

They once again set out for Syria and met the person from Nisibis. They stayed with him for a long time until he too passed away, and before his death, he advised that they should go to a certain monk residing in Amuriyah (Syria).

They went to Amuriyah and settled with the monk there. They also worked and eventually became owners of herds of cows and goats. After some time, this devout monk also fell ill and passed away.

Sayyidina Salman (may Allah be pleased with him) was very saddened by this and, bidding him farewell, said:

"O righteous person! Now whom do you advise me to go to?"

The good man replied:

"O Salman! By Allah, I do not think there is anyone among the people now who is at our level that you should go to." He meant that people had changed and altered the religion.

Then he said:

"Yes! The time for the advent of a prophet has come. He will be sent with the religion of Ibrahim (peace be upon him). He will arise from the land of the Arabs and then migrate from his city (Makkah) to a region between two black, stony valleys. There will be abundant dates there. This prophet will have certain signs that will not be hidden from anyone. He will accept gifts but will not eat from charity. There will be the seal of prophethood between his two shoulders. When you see him, you will recognize him. If you can reach this land of the Arabs, then go."

Then that righteous person also passed away and was buried.

Sayyidina Salman (may Allah be pleased with him) stayed in Amuriyah as long as Allah willed. He was now searching for someone or a caravan that would take him to the land of prophethood. He waited continuously until one day, a caravan from the tribe of Banu Kalb (Hijaz) passed by, who were traders. Sayyidina Salman (may Allah be pleased with him) requested them to take him with them to their land, offering his herds of cows and goats in return.

They agreed. So Sayyidina Salman (may Allah be pleased with him) gave them his herds, and they took him with them. When they reached Wadi al-Qura, greed and covetousness took hold of their hearts. They oppressed him and claimed that he was their purchased slave. They then sold him to a Jew.

Sayyidina Salman (may Allah be pleased with him) was unable to defend himself and began serving the Jew as a slave. One day, a man from the Jewish tribe of Banu Qurayza in Madinah came to the Jew; he was the Jew's paternal cousin. He bought Sayyidina Salman (may Allah be pleased with him) and took him to Madinah.

When Sayyidina Salman (may Allah be pleased with him) saw Madinah, its date palms, and its stones, he became certain that this was the land of prophethood described by the monk from Amuriyah. He settled there with peace of mind and began waiting for the person who would assume the position of prophethood. Many years passed in this way. Allah Almighty sent His Messenger (peace be upon him). The Prophet (peace be upon him) resided in Makkah Mukarramah as a prophet for a period (thirteen years) and engaged in calling and preaching. During this entire time, Sayyidina Salman (may Allah be pleased with him) did not hear any mention of him. This was because he was constantly engaged in the service of his Jewish master day and night.

Then the Prophet (peace be upon him) migrated to Madinah Munawwarah. The Prophet (peace be upon him) was residing in Madinah Munawwarah, but Sayyidina Salman (may Allah be pleased with him) had no news about him. One day, he was climbing a date palm in his master's orchard, busy with his work. His master was sitting under that palm when a Jewish man from his paternal cousins (tribe) came there, stood beside him, and began saying:

"Oh my friend! May Allah destroy the people of Banu Aws and Banu Khazraj. They are all gathered around a man in Quba who has come from Makkah Mukarramah and claims to be the Prophet of Allah."

As soon as Sayyidina Salman (may Allah be pleased with him) heard this, his whole body shuddered. A thrill overcame him. His heart leapt with joy as if it wanted to fly into the air. He trembled on the date palm and nearly fell, but he managed to steady himself. He immediately descended from the palm and shouted at the man:

"What are you saying? What news are you giving?"

Seeing his state, his master became angry with him. He extended his hand and gave him a hard slap on the face, saying:

"What concern do you have with this man? Why are you interested in this news? Go and mind your own business!"

Sayyidina Salman (may Allah be pleased with him) remained silent and climbed back up the date palm to continue his work. Although he was occupied with work, his heart was fixed on the news of the prophethood. He wanted to meet this prophet as soon as possible and confirm the qualities described by the monk from Amuriyah:

"He will accept gifts but will not eat from charity. There will be the seal of prophethood between his two shoulders."

When night fell, he gathered all the food and drink he had and set out to visit the Prophet (peace be upon him). He arrived to meet the Prophet (peace be upon him) while the Prophet (peace be upon him) was sitting in a place in Quba. When Sayyidina Salman (may Allah be pleased with him) entered the presence of the Prophet (peace be upon him), he saw a considerable number of people gathered around him.

As soon as he entered, he began to say, "I have heard that you people are strangers here. You must be in need, and I have these food items which I had kept with the intention of giving in charity. Now I am bringing them for this purpose." Then Sayyidina Salman (may Allah be pleased with him) presented the items to the Prophet (peace be upon him) and sat aside to observe what the Prophet (peace be upon him) would do with them.

The Prophet (peace be upon him) looked at the food items and then turned his attention to his companions (may Allah be pleased with them) and said:

"You may eat," the Prophet (peace be upon him) said. But the Prophet (peace be upon him) did not extend his hand and did not eat any of it.

When Sayyidina Salman (may Allah be pleased with him) saw this, he said to himself: "By Allah! One of the attributes of the prophet who is to be sent is that 'he will not eat from charity.'" Now, only the confirmation of the other two attributes remained. He then returned to his master.

A few days later, he gathered some food and drink again and went to the Prophet (peace be upon him). He greeted the Prophet (peace be upon him) and said:

"I have seen that you do not eat from charity. But these items are a gift which I have brought in honor of you and wish to present to you. They are not charity." Saying this, he presented the items to the Prophet (peace be upon him).

The Prophet (peace be upon him) extended his blessed hand and ate some of it. His companions (may Allah be pleased with them) also ate some as desired. When Sayyidina Salman (may Allah be pleased with him) saw this, he said to himself: "This is the second attribute of the sent prophet." Now only one thing remained, which was to see the seal of prophethood between his shoulders.

But it was not easy for him to do this. Sayyidina Salman (may Allah be pleased with him) then returned to his master. However, his heart was waiting to get accurate information about the Prophet (peace be upon him). He waited for a few days and then set out to find the Prophet (peace be upon him).

This time he found him in the cemetery of Madinah Munawwarah, Al-Baqi' al-Gharqad. The Prophet (peace be upon him) was there stopping for the burial of an Ansari companion. When Salman (may

Allah be pleased with him) arrived, he found the companions (may Allah be pleased with them) around the Prophet (peace be upon him).

The Prophet (peace be upon him) was dressed in two garments. One was tied as an izar (a lower garment) and the other was worn as a qamis (shirt), similar to how an ihram is worn.

Sayyidina Salman (may Allah be pleased with him) greeted the Prophet (peace be upon him) and then focused his gaze on the Prophet's back (between his shoulders) to see if he could spot the seal of prophethood that had been described by the monk of Amoria. When the Prophet (peace be upon him) saw him moving around, he understood that this person was trying to see and verify what he had been told about. The Prophet (peace be upon him) shifted his shoulders and deliberately let his cloak fall from his back. Sayyidina Salman (may Allah be pleased with him) saw the seal of prophethood with his own eyes and became certain. Immediately, he rushed forward, kissed it, and began to weep profusely.

Seeing his condition, the Prophet (peace be upon him) told him, "Come forward and sit in front of me." He moved forward and sat in front of the blessed face of the Prophet (peace be upon him). The Prophet (peace be upon him) asked him about the story. He recounted his entire story.

He told the Prophet (peace be upon him) that he had been a wealthy and prosperous young man. In search of the truth and the wealth of faith, he had discarded all honor and power. He had moved from one monk to another, serving them and learning religion from them. Eventually, he ended up as a purchased slave in the service of a Jewish man in Madinah Munawwarah.

Sayyidina Salman (may Allah be pleased with him) then began to look at the Prophet (peace be upon him) with devotion and respect. Tears of overwhelming love streamed from his eyes, wetting his cheeks and falling to the ground.

He was filled with immense joy and happiness and was experiencing great glad tidings. Then he embraced Islam, recited the Shahada, and went back to his Jewish master. The Jewish master increased his workload and service requirements. While the companions of the Prophet (peace be upon him) returned to the Prophet's service, Sayyidina Salman (may Allah be pleased with him) was deprived of this honor due to his bondage. He was also unable to participate in the Battle of Badr and the Battle of Uhud. When the Prophet (peace be upon him) saw his condition, he said:

"O Salman! Negotiate with your master for the price and terms of your freedom. That is, agree on a price for your freedom and free yourself from this Jewish master."

When Sayyidina Salman (may Allah be pleased with him) discussed this with his master, the master set a very high price for his freedom. He demanded forty uqiya of silver (sixteen hundred dirhams) in addition to the condition that three hundred date palms be collected, planted, and irrigated. Furthermore, he stipulated that these three hundred date palms must grow lush and thrive before he would grant freedom.

When Sayyidina Salman (may Allah be pleased with him) mentioned the compensation and conditions demanded by the Jewish master to the Prophet (peace be upon him), the Prophet (peace be upon him) instructed his companions to assist Salman in acquiring the date palms. The Muslims cooperated fully, with each person bringing date palms from their own orchards according to their means. When three hundred saplings were collected, the Prophet (peace be upon him) addressed Sayyidina Salman (may Allah be pleased with him) and said:

"O Salman! Now go and dig the holes for planting. And when it is time to plant the saplings, do not plant them yourself. Instead, come and inform me when the holes are ready."

Sayyidina Salman (may Allah be pleased with him) began preparing the holes. The companions also assisted him in digging the holes until three hundred holes were made for the saplings. He then came to the Prophet (peace be upon him) and reported that the holes were ready for planting. The Prophet (peace be upon him) went with him to the planting site. The companions placed the date saplings near the Prophet (peace be upon him), and he himself planted them in the holes with his blessed hands.

Sayyidina Salman (may Allah be pleased with him) swears by Allah that none of those saplings dried up; rather, all three hundred saplings grew green and thrived. When he gave these date palms to the Jewish master, only the cash payment remained. One day, some gold was brought to the Prophet (peace be upon him) as part of the spoils of war from some expeditions. He addressed his companions and said:

"This gold is for the Persian slave to fulfill his agreement for freedom. Leave it for him."

When Sayyidina Salman (may Allah be pleased with him) came, the Prophet (peace be upon him) told him:

"O Salman! Take this gold and pay off the amount specified in your agreement for freedom."

Sayyidina Salman (may Allah be pleased with him) took the gold and paid the required amount to the Jewish master, thus securing his freedom. From that day until his (peace be upon him) death, he continued to serve the Prophet (peace be upon him) and enjoyed his companionship and blessings.

(Musnad Ahmad: 7/613, Hadith: 23385, 7/882, Hadith: 24138; Al-Mawardi in "A'lam al-Nubuwwah" [p. 337] has deemed the narrators of this hadith as reliable, Majma' al-Zawa'id: 9/336; Sirah A'lam al-Nubala': 1/510; Shu'ayb al-Arna'ut also considered its chain of transmission strong)

The Key to Sin

Someone said to me:

I had a very close friend who was like a brother to me. He was killed in an accident last week. My prayer to Allah is that He may have mercy on him and pardon his deeds. The difficulty is not that he has died, because we all have to die one day.

The difficulty is that our friend was very experienced with the Internet. He had a great skill in revealing websites and sites containing nudity and pornographic content. In fact, he had created his own site with pornographic images and movies. He had a group of people in his circle who were registered on his site. He used to send new pornographic images and movies to their email addresses from time to time.

The person suddenly died. And now the problem is that we do not know the secret number (Password) of his site to shut it down or take any action. I was thinking about these matters and at the same time waiting to perform his funeral prayer in the mosque. I had walked to the mosque with the funeral. He was in the form of a body carried on the shoulders of others. I was wondering what he would see in his grave now. Would he face those naked pictures? "Sufficient for us is Allah, and He is the best disposer of affairs."

After the funeral prayer, we had now reached the cemetery, where there were graves all around in extreme desolation. There was a crowd of people around him. I peered into his grave. Ah! What would his state be in it? I saw some people crying.

I thought to myself, could their crying benefit him? We buried him. Then we left him alone in that dark grave. His family and wealth all returned. Now only his own deeds remained with him!

You cannot imagine what his deeds were. His mother had a dream where some boys were urinating on his grave. She was asking for the interpretation of this dream. Poor woman, what does she know about what her son was secretly doing?

I also heard about this dream. I said to myself:

This dream does not need any interpretation. Its meaning is absolutely clear. The boys who are urinating on his grave are the same ones to whom he used to send those images and films. Moreover, they had started sending those images to others they knew. What a terrible matter! How will that person endure the sins of these people? Because the hadith says:

"Whoever calls to misguidance will have upon him the same burden of sin as those who follow him, without diminishing their sins in any way." (Mukhtasar Sahih Muslim: 60 18)

I tried my best to do good for my deceased friend and cut off the seeds of evil he had sown. So I contacted the hosting company of that site and requested them to terminate the subscription. But they declined to take any action.

In fact, they did not even believe me that the person had died because I did not know the secret numbers with which he had booked that site. I shouted, cried out, and made a lot of noise, saying, "People! That person has died." But none of them was willing to heed my words. I sat and began to think about his condition.

I recalled the saying of the Prophet Muhammad (peace be upon him):

"There are people among men who are keys to good and locks to evil, and there are people among men who are keys to evil and locks to good. Glad tidings to those whom Allah makes keys to good, and woe to those whom Allah makes keys to evil." (Sahih al-Jami: 2223)

I think he was one of such people. I had admonished him a lot and forbade him, saying, "How will you bear the sins of others? Why do you become the key to sin? How will you bear the burden of other people's sins on the Day of Judgment?" But he did not take any notice of my words. He thought he was young and just wanted to have fun and enjoy himself. He considered all these matters to be mere amusement and pastime. I seek refuge in Allah. How many young people have watched naked images (films) and eventually become involved in obscenity and fornication? Similarly, how many maidens have become involved in such evils? That person has died. But on the Day of Judgment, he will be held accountable for every gaze and what he saw from them. And there will be inquiry about all others as well. He will be held accountable for every act of obscenity and fornication in which he was involved and others were involved. And there will be reckoning for every image (and film) he disseminated or others contributed to its promotion and expansion.

I do not know how long and to what extent he will be forced to bear the sins of others. But I wish that Allah pardons his sins. And Allah is Sufficient for us, and He is the Best Disposer of affairs.

Obstruction to the Rain of Mercy

In the time of Prophet Moses (peace be upon him), the Children of Israel faced a severe drought. The people gathered around Prophet Moses (peace be upon him) and said:

"O Prophet, who has the honor of speaking with Allah! Pray to your Lord for us that He sends down rain and provides us with water."

Prophet Moses (peace be upon him) stood up with them and went towards a desert. At that time, their number was seventy thousand or more. They all gathered in the presence of Allah and began to pray. They were disheveled and in a state of poverty, hungry and thirsty.

Prophet Moses (peace be upon him) started praying:

"O Allah! Grant us rain. Shower us with Your mercy and have mercy on us through the infants, the mute animals, and the elderly with bent backs."

Not a single drop of water fell from the sky. Instead, the drought increased, and the heat and intensity of the sun intensified.

Prophet Moses (peace be upon him) prayed again: "O Allah! Grant us rain of mercy!" Allah responded:

"Why should I grant you rain, when among you is a person who has been openly challenging Me with sins for forty years? Announce among the people that this person should leave your midst, for it is because of him that I have withheld the rain from you."

Prophet Moses (peace be upon him) announced to his people:

"O disobedient one, who has been challenging Allah with disobedience for forty years, leave our midst. It is only because of you that the rain has been withheld from us."

The disobedient person looked to his right and left but found no one leaving the gathering. He was now certain that he himself was the one being sought!

He said to himself:

"If I leave this gathering, I will be disgraced and humiliated in the eyes of the entire Children of Israel. And if I remain out of shame, these people will remain deprived of rain because of me." He was deeply distressed by this thought, and tears began to flow from his eyes. In his regret, he hid his face in his clothes (collar) and prayed to Allah:

"O Allah! O my Master and Lord! I have disobeyed You for forty years. Nevertheless, You have covered my sins and granted me respite. Now I come to Your court with my head bowed in submission, as Your obedient servant. Accept my presence."

He then began to weep and implore before his Creator and Master. Before he could complete his plea, a white cloud rose up, appeared in the middle of the sky, and began to pour down rain with such force as if water skins had been opened.

Prophet Moses (peace be upon him) was astonished at this and said to his Lord:

"O Allah! You have granted us rain, even though no one among us has left."

Allah said:

"O Moses! I have granted you rain because of the tears of repentance of that person who had been challenging Me with sins. It is because of him that I had withheld the rain from you."

Prophet Moses (peace be upon him) said: "O Allah! Show me this obedient and repentant servant!"

Allah replied:

"O Moses! I did not humiliate this servant when he was disobedient. Shall I now disgrace him before people when he has humbled himself and become obedient before Me?"

Bold Decision

Saidina Tufayl bin Amr al-Dawsi (may Allah be pleased with him) was a beloved leader of his tribe, Banu Daws. Everyone listened to him and obeyed him. One day, he came to Makkah for some need. When he entered the city, the leaders of Quraysh saw him and gathered around him.

They asked him: "Who are you?"

He replied: "I am Tufayl bin Amr, the chief of the Banu Daws tribe." They looked at each other with meaningful glances. They feared that if the Prophet (peace be upon him) saw him, he would invite him to Islam and preach. If this leader embraced Islam, Islam would gain strength. They all gathered around him.

One of them said:

"There is a man in Makkah who considers himself a prophet. Avoid sitting with him and listening to him. He is a magician. If you listen to him, know that he will corrupt your intellect."

Another leader echoed similar sentiments, and a third one spoke even more negatively. They all engaged in strong propaganda against the Prophet Muhammad (peace be upon him).

Saidina Tufayl (may Allah be pleased with him) says: "By Allah! They continued to scare me about the Prophet (peace be upon him), scaring me until I made a firm resolve in my heart not to listen to him or speak to him. I even stuffed cotton into my ears so that not a single word from his speech would accidentally enter my ears."

The next morning, I went to the Masjid al-Haram and saw the Messenger of Allah (peace be upon him) standing near the Kaaba, praying. I stood very close to him. Despite my best efforts not to, Allah made me hear some words from his blessed tongue. I heard very beautiful speech. I then said to myself:

"May my mother lose me! By Allah, I am a person of reason and insight. I know how to distinguish between good and bad. What obstacle is there for me to listen to this person? If his words are good, I will accept them, and if they are bad, I will reject them." So, I stayed there until he finished his prayer.

When the Prophet (peace be upon him) stood up and headed towards his home, I followed him until he entered his house. I also entered behind him and said:

"O Muhammad (peace be upon him)! Your people have told me such and such things about you. By Allah, they continuously scared me about you until I stuffed cotton in my ears so that I wouldn't hear anything from you. Yet, I have heard some very beautiful words from you. Now, present your message clearly to me."

Upon hearing this, the blessed face of the Prophet (peace be upon him) brightened with joy. He was very happy and, with pleasure, presented the invitation to Islam to Saidina Tufayl (may Allah be pleased with him) and recited some verses from the Quran.

Saidina Tufayl (may Allah be pleased with him) began to reflect on his situation. He realized that he was drifting further away from Allah every day. He worshipped stone idols that could not hear or respond to him. Now the truth was clearly before him.

Saidina Tufayl (may Allah be pleased with him) started to think about the consequences of embracing Islam. How would he change his own and his ancestors' religion? What would people say about him? The life of luxury he enjoyed, the wealth he had accumulated, his family, wife, children, neighbors, and friends—everything seemed to be at stake.

He remained silent for a while, contemplating and comparing his worldly life with the Hereafter. Suddenly, he cast aside his worldly attachments. He placed all his comforts and luxuries under his feet. Yes! He decided to adopt steadfastness and perseverance in the religion of Islam. He resolved to disregard those who were pleased and to ignore the discontent of those who were displeased. If Allah, the Lord of the heavens, was pleased with him, he cared nothing for the displeasure of the people of the earth.

My wealth and possessions are in the hands of the Lord of the heavens.

My health and illness are under the control of the Lord of the heavens.

My status, position, and prestige are gifts from the Lord of the heavens.

Indeed, even my life and death are in the hands of the Lord of the heavens.

Since the Lord of the heavens is pleased with me, I care not about what I have lost of worldly possessions. If Allah loves me, then whoever is displeased with me or criticizes me, so be it. Whoever mocks or ridicules me, let them do so.

As the poet said:

Oh, that you would be sweet and pleasant for me, though the rest of the world remains bitter!

Oh, that you would be pleased with me, though the entire creation remains displeased with me!

O that the relationship between you and me were established and that the rest of the worlds, even if they were in discord with me, remained so.

If your love is genuine, then everything else becomes easy. All that is above the earth will eventually turn to dust.

Indeed, Saidina Tufayl (may Allah be pleased with him) embraced Islam right there and declared the testimony of faith. His courage increased greatly, and his determination and resolve became strong.

He said to the Prophet (peace be upon him):

"O Prophet of Allah (peace be upon him)! I am the leader and guide of my people; they all obey and follow me. Now I will return to them and invite them to Islam."

Saidina Tufayl (may Allah be pleased with him) then left Mecca and headed swiftly towards his people. His heart was filled with the passion for spreading the message of Islam. He crossed the mountains and valleys in his path until he reached the territory of his people.

When he entered his residence, the first person to come to him was his father, an elderly man.

Saidina Tufayl (may Allah be pleased with him) immediately said to him:

"O Father! Now our paths are separate. I am no longer related to you, nor are you related to me!"

The father asked: "My son, what is this all about?"

Saidina Tufayl (may Allah be pleased with him) replied:

"I have embraced Islam and have started following and adhering to the religion of Prophet Muhammad (peace be upon him)."

His father said: "My son, my religion is also the same as yours."

Saidina Tufayl (may Allah be pleased with him) asked him to go, perform ablution, and wear clean clothes so that he could teach him the knowledge he had acquired. The father complied, went, and returned after performing ablution and dressing in clean clothes. Saidina Tufayl (may Allah be pleased with him) then invited him to Islam, and he embraced it.

Then Saidina Tufayl (may Allah be pleased with him) went to his home. When his wife came to him, he told her the same thing: "Stay away from me, from now on our paths are separate. I am no longer related to you, nor are you related to me."

She responded:

My parents are devoted to you. What is the reason?

He replied that Islam has caused separation and division between us, while I have embraced the religion of Prophet Muhammad (peace be upon him).

Upon this, she said:

"My religion is the same as yours." To this, Saidina Tufayl (may Allah be pleased with him) commanded her to go, perform ablution and purification, and then return to him. She immediately left and went.

She had an idol named "Dhual-Shara" which they revered and believed would punish those who abandoned its worship. She was afraid that if she converted to Islam, this idol might harm her and her children. Therefore, she returned to him and said:

"May my parents be sacrificed for you! Are you not afraid for your children from Dhual-Shara?"

Saidina Tufayl (may Allah be pleased with him) replied:

"Go, and I guarantee you that Dhual-Shara will not harm our children." She went, performed ablution, and returned to him. He invited her to Islam, and she too embraced it.

Now Saidina Tufayl (may Allah be pleased with him) started going around his people, visiting house to house, and inviting them to Islam. He would enter their gatherings and meetings, and meet them on their paths. But they refused to embrace Islam and abandon the worship of Dhual-Shara. Saidina Tufayl (may Allah be pleased with him) became angry and departed for Makkah. There, he presented himself to Prophet Muhammad (peace be upon him) and said:

"O Messenger of Allah (peace be upon him)! My tribe, Banu Daws, has disobeyed my command and refused to listen to me. O Messenger of Allah (peace be upon him)! Please make a supplication against them." Upon hearing this, the color of the Prophet's (peace be upon him) face changed. He raised both hands towards the sky. Saidina Tufayl (may Allah be pleased with him) thought that the Prophet (peace be upon him) was making a supplication against them, and he thought to himself that Banu Daws was doomed!

But the compassionate Prophet and mercy to the worlds (peace be upon him) began to make this supplication:

"O Allah! Guide Banu Daws. O Allah! Grant guidance to the tribe of Banu Daws."

Then he (peace be upon him) turned towards Saidina Tufayl (may Allah be pleased with him) and commanded him:

"Return to your people and invite them to Islam. But do this with great love and gentleness." Thus, he returned to his tribe. He continued inviting them until all the people of the tribe embraced Islam.

Time continued to pass, many nights and days went by. The Prophet Muhammad (peace be upon him) departed from this worldly life to the eternal life. But Saidina Tufayl (may Allah be pleased with him) remained steadfast in Islam even after the Prophet's (peace be upon him) death. He eventually drank the cup of martyrdom in the Battle of Yamama!

(Al-Isabah Fi Tamyiz Al-Sahabah by Ibn Hajar: 3/521)

A Young Man

———

A young man, who was only sixteen years old, was sitting in the mosque reciting the Quran. He was waiting for the Iqamah (call to commence the prayer) for Fajr prayer. When the Iqamah for the prayer began, he rolled up the Quran and placed it in its place, and stood up in the row. Suddenly, the young man collapsed and fell unconscious. The other worshippers picked him up and took him to the hospital. The doctor who examined him informed me that the young man was brought to us lying on a bed like a living corpse. When I checked him, I found that blood had clotted in the arteries of his brain. His condition was at such a stage that if a camel had reached this stage, it would have died. I observed the young man closely and realized that he was on the brink of death and taking his last breaths.

We made every effort to help him and provide vitality and freshness to his heart. I had the first aid specialist doctor standing by his side who was providing deep care for him, while I went to get medical instruments for his treatment. When I hurriedly returned, I saw that the young man had grabbed the first aid specialist doctor's hand, and the doctor had placed his ear close to the young man's mouth.

The young man was whispering something in the doctor's ear in a very faint voice. For a few moments, I stood at a distance observing them. Suddenly, the young man released the doctor's hand. We made every effort to have him lie on his side. Then he said in a heavy voice:

"I bear witness that there is no deity but Allah, and I bear witness that Muhammad is His servant and messenger."

He began repeating this testimony of faith repeatedly. His pulse was fading, and his heartbeat seemed to be disappearing. We were engaged in efforts to save him, but Allah's decree was decisive and stronger. The young man passed away. As soon as his last breath ended, the first aid specialist doctor began to weep uncontrollably. So much so that he could no longer stand on his feet and sat down in his place. We were very surprised by his condition. We asked him: "O so-and-so! What is the matter? Why are you crying? This is not the first time you have seen a dying person's body." Yet the doctor continued to sob and weep.

When his grief and crying subsided somewhat, we asked him: "What was the young man whispering in your ear during his final moments?"

He replied:

"Doctor, when he saw you rushing here and there, giving orders to one thing and another, he realized that you were his primary doctor. Then he told me: 'Doctor, tell my fellow heart specialist doctor not to trouble himself and others with running around. I am about to die. By Allah, I am already seeing my place in paradise.'"

O heedless one! Worry about the Hereafter, it is nothing.

Do not be deceived; the pleasures of this world are nothing.

Life is but a few days; it is nothing.

Nothing at all, and its trustworthiness is nothing.

You are for worship; remember that.

Not for pride and arrogance, remember that.

Otherwise, shame and regret will follow; remember that.

Life is but a few days; remember that.

Even if you have attained a high position, so what?

Even if you have acquired wealth and riches, so what?

Even if you have built a magnificent palace, so what?

Even if you have displayed your grandeur, so what?

One day, death is inevitable, after all, death is certain.

Do whatever you have to do, after all, death is certain.

At the Threshold of Death

═══

She wrote her autobiography with her own hands. She says that there is no day that passes without her crying. I think about committing suicide many times each day. My life no longer seems to have any value in my eyes. I spend every moment yearning for death. I wish I had never been born and had never seen this world.

The beginning of my autobiography with a friend goes like this: She invited me to her house. My friend is one of those who use the internet extensively.

She ignited my desire and interest in seeing, knowing, and enjoying this world. She taught me in just about two months how to use the internet. My fascination reached the point where I began visiting her house frequently. I learned to communicate directly with her. I also learned how to turn on the computer and how to access the internet. During these two months, I was constantly fighting with my husband to get an internet connection at home. But he was against it.

I even convinced him by saying that I feel very lonely and extremely bored after he leaves for work, especially since we are away from family. I also argued that all my friends have internet connections and use them. Why shouldn't I use it and chat with them through it, especially since it is much cheaper than the telephone? Eventually, my husband agreed. But I wish that had not happened!

I started chatting with my friends daily. After that, my husband had no complaints or concerns about me. As soon as he left for work, I would eagerly rush to the internet. I would spend several hours sitting on it. I even started wishing that my husband would stay out as much as possible. I love my husband, and he has never neglected any matter concerning me.

It is true that his financial situation was somewhat weaker compared to my sisters and friends. But he works hard and does his best for my happiness. As time passed, I began to feel that the internet was becoming more and more a source of entertainment for me. My condition reached a point where I had no interest in going to meet my parents. Previously, we used to visit both my parental home and in-laws every fifteen days.

Whenever my husband would suddenly come home, I would get flustered and I would hastily close everything on the internet in such a frenzy that it would amaze him. But he had no suspicions about me. In fact, he wanted to see what I did on the internet and how I entertained myself with it.

It might just be a trivial feeling or perhaps it is jealousy that one day when he heard someone's voice during a live chat, which I could not hide from him despite all my efforts and precautions. After that day, he would occasionally show displeasure towards me. And he would say that the internet is a vast field for acquiring information. But it is also a cause of wasting time.

Time passed and I became more and more infatuated with chatting with new people every day. I had shifted the issue of raising and nurturing the children to the maid. I already knew when my husband would come home. Therefore, I would turn off the computer and internet before he arrived. As far as I am concerned, I began to neglect my grooming and appearance.

Before getting into the internet, I would make myself look good and well-groomed when my husband came home, but now my grooming had gradually disappeared. I was so obsessed with the internet that I would quietly sneak into the internet computer room after my husband had gone to sleep and would sneak back into bed before he woke up. After a while, he might have realized that I was wasting time on the internet without reason. But he pitied me because I was alone, away from my parents and siblings!

And I took great unfair advantage of his compassionate feelings. He would be upset that I was neglecting the children. Over this issue, he had scolded me several times. To which I would pretend to cry and tell him that you don't know what happens at home after you leave. I take great care of them. I spend a lot of time on their upbringing and nurturing. But they exhaust me with their mischief all day!

In short, I became indifferent to everything, even to my husband! Previously, I used to call him dozens of times when he was out of the house and just wanted to hear his voice. Now that the internet had stepped into the house and entered my life, he could no longer hear my voice, except when there was a specific need for something in the house, and then occasionally, I would call.

Now my husband became very jealous and angry about the internet. Six months passed in this state. I had formed relationships with people under several fake names. I didn't even know whether those names were for men or women. I would start conversations with whoever spoke to me through chatting, even though I knew that the person talking was a man.

Yes! There was one person I became very much inclined towards. I liked talking to him. I enjoyed his witty conversation, jokes, and puns. His talks were very interesting and delightful. Days went by, and our mutual relationship deepened more and more.

It took three months to establish this relationship. He drew me towards him with his sweet talk. Every word of his conversation was overflowing with love and affection. My desire to see him grew stronger. Perhaps his words were not that beautiful, but the devil kept presenting them in an alluring way before me. Until now, all our conversations had been through chatting, only verbally.

One day he demanded to hear my voice, which I rejected. He insisted strongly. Until he started threatening that if I didn't provide my voice, he would also stop written conversations, neither chatting nor emailing.

I made a great effort to avoid his demand and to stand firm on my opinion. But I could not hold out. I don't know why. Eventually, I agreed to voice conversations with a few conditions. We agreed that there would be only one conversation by voice.

Now we opted for voice conversations. Although the required system was not very standard, his voice was very sweet and his conversation was extremely charming and captivating.

One day he told me that my voice was not coming through clearly on the internet. So, he asked for my phone number. I refused him. I was very surprised by his audacity, while I could not even muster the courage to talk to him for long. I swear by Allah, I was certain that the accursed devil was controlling me. He was presenting his voice in an enticing way and wanted to steal my religion, morality, and chastity, waging a war against them. Eventually, the day came when I spoke to him on the phone. From that day, deviation and misguidance began in my life. I gradually went very far down the wrong path. The devil led me far astray. I won't prolong the discussion about this matter.

Anyone who reads my story might think that my husband was indifferent towards me. That he was often absent from home. No! The reality is quite the opposite. He used to keep to his work and would come straight home from there. He rarely went to his friends' places for my sake and for the sake of our children.

With the passage of time and the rotation of days and nights, I continued to gain increasing expertise in the internet, and my obsession with it grew. I would spend 8 to 12 hours daily on the internet. I began to dislike my husband being at home too much. In fact, I had even criticized him several times. I started advising him and encouraging him to take up part-time work so that we could get rid of our debts and free ourselves from the endless cycle of installment payments.

He agreed to my suggestion and became a partner in a small business run by one of his friends. After that, I spent even more time on the internet. Occasionally, he would be shocked by the telephone and internet connection bills, which sometimes amounted to thousands of riyals. But he was unable to stop me from my internet usage.

My relationship with my acquaintance grew deeper day by day. When he had heard my voice several times, and had listened to it thoroughly, he began demanding to see me. I didn't really care about his demand, nor did I consider ending our relationship. Instead, I would express my displeasure and frustration over his request. In reality, I was even more eager to see him. But I remained slightly aloof, not because of any particular reason, but simply out of fear and distant apprehensions prevented me from granting him permission.

His insistence grew stronger each day. He only wanted to see me, nothing else. I accepted his demand with the condition that this meeting would be the first and last one. We made this vow to each other and then met in a market. And between us was also the third accursed devil. The truth is that I was captivated by him at first sight. In fact, the devil had decorated him well in my eyes.

My husband was not unattractive. But the devil presents the forbidden in an alluring way. We both went our separate ways after the meeting. However, after that encounter, our relationship grew stronger and stronger. He did not know that I was married and had children. Afterward, he saw and met me several times.

Gradually, he learned everything about me. He placed me in a position where I began to hate my husband. Eventually, he suggested that I get a divorce from my husband so that he could marry me.

I had begun to hate my husband. I started creating new problems daily to somehow force him to divorce me. My husband could not tolerate these despicable matters. Therefore, he started spending more and more time away from home. Until one day, this tragedy occurred.

One day, my husband informed me that he was going on a five-day business trip. He advised me to visit my family with the children. I felt this was the perfect time to meet my acquaintance openly. I refused to go to my family. Reluctantly, my husband agreed. Then, on Friday, he left for his five-day trip. After his departure, we scheduled a meeting for Sunday. I promised this devilish person that I would meet him in a market. I got into his car, and he drove me around various streets.

It was my first time going out with a stranger, so I was somewhat anxious and worried. He seemed even more anxious than I was. I told him that I couldn't stay out too long. I feared that my husband might call or something else might happen. He responded that if your husband finds out, what's the worst that could happen? He might divorce you, and you'd be free. I didn't like his words and tone. I became even more worried. I told him not to go too far; I didn't want to be late coming home. He then started distracting me with irrelevant talk. Suddenly, I found myself in an unfamiliar place, which seemed dark. It looked like a garden or a farmhouse. I started shouting at him, asking what kind of place this was and where he was taking me.

A few moments later, the car stopped, and another person opened my side of the door and roughly dragged me out of the car. A third person was still inside the farmhouse, and I saw a fourth person sitting there. Strange smells were coming from the place. Everything felt like a shock to me. I screamed, cried, and begged them for mercy and compassion. Out of sheer terror, I couldn't understand what was happening around me. Then I felt a hard slap on my face. A voice was yelling at me. The voice and the slap not only shocked me but made me lose my senses due to fear and panic.

What happened to me after that is a different story. After a while, when I regained consciousness, I was deeply traumatized. I was trembling all over, and I couldn't stop crying for a moment. They blindfolded me, put me into the car, and dropped me near my house.

I rushed into my home. My only task now was to cry and continue crying until the tears dried up. I stayed in my room all the time and didn't even meet my children. I hadn't eaten anything. I had developed a hatred for myself. I attempted suicide. Even though I was at home, I didn't know anything about my children or feel their presence.

When my husband returned from his trip, my condition was so bad that he forcibly took me to the hospital. The doctors gave me comfortable, soothing, and strong medications. I pleaded with my husband to take me to my family as soon as possible. I cried continuously, and my family couldn't do anything. They thought that there was a conflict between me and my husband for some reason.

My father tried to reach an understanding with my husband, but they did not come to any conclusion. Because my husband was actually unaware of anything, and no one else knew about the tragedy that befell me. Even my family took me to a healer suddenly, thinking that I might be ill.

In short, I was no longer worthy of my husband. Therefore, I demanded a divorce from him. God is a witness that I did this only out of respect and honor for him. Because I was no longer deserving of living among people of dignity and honor.

I have dug my own grave with my own hands. And the person who got to know me through internet chat is not my friend; rather, he was a predator who preyed on girls who chat.

My husband was deeply distressed and sorrowful about my condition. In fact, for several days, he left all his work so that he could stay with me. He refused to give me a divorce. He loved me with all his heart. He made a great effort for my sake. He even started a family and a home. Now he did not want to destroy all of this.

I kept my secret buried in my chest. Now, every passing day brings even more torment upon me. What humiliation have those vile people subjected me to?

How did I become a heap of garbage in front of those who drink alcohol and use drugs, so that they could tear my body apart as they wished? How foolish and ignorant was I?

Why did I waste several months redirecting my loving feelings towards him, when he did not deserve them?

Now I am writing these words while lying on a sickbed, which may become my deathbed!

The Story of Ahmed

There was a brother who came overseas to seek a bachelor's degree. This was the first time he got freedom from his family and society, where people were very religious and very practicing.

He comes to a place like England. He's in a free-mixing university and a society where girls look at you. In fact, in his society there were no girls in your class. Now, all of a sudden, they're sitting next to him, and he can actually find an excuse to talk to them. "Hey, can I borrow a pen?" "Hey, can I borrow some paper?" And conversation becomes very easy.

Now he was flipping up for them. This was the reality that he went through. He came from a foreign land, and this attraction hit him right away. The initial stages were that he would just go out for lunch, just go out for meetings, and that is how life continued. He never actually committed zina.

But one day, he went to a party and he committed zina out of pure emotion. He committed zina, and when he was done, he just lay there thinking, "I have just ruined myself." He didn't know what to do. He didn't know where to go. He didn't have any close friends that could guide him. He knew that the only place that had the guidance he had known was back in his hometown.

He booked a ticket back to Saudi Arabia, where he was from. On his way, he had a stopover in the country of Qatar. While he was in Qatar, he went to the mosque and was just crying.

One of the students of Sheikh Ibn Baz, may Allah have mercy on him, saw this man and went up to him and said, "Young man, why are you crying? What's wrong?"

He explained the situation: "I committed a sin and I've destroyed myself. The only way I can get rid of this pain is if I go back and have the hudud (Islamic punishment for Zina) implemented on me. This is the only way I will be purified." The student calms the man down and says, "Look, don't do anything rash. Let's go back to Riyadh together and we'll deal with the situation."

They head back to Riyadh, and the man is still crying throughout the whole journey. He feels really bad for what he has done. The student says, "Look, we've arrived in Riyadh. Go spend the night at home. I will call you in the morning. Just make sure you don't do anything. Don't do anything, just wait till I call you."

The next morning, the student calls Sheikh Ibn Baz and asks, "Sheikh, this is what happened. I met this man. He committed zina, and he feels that the only way he can be purified is if he has the hudud implemented on him."

Sheikh Ibn Baz says, "Tell this man not to turn himself in. Rather, this sin has been hidden from the people. Continue to hide it. Instead seek forgiveness from Allah Subhanahu wa Ta'ala and turn yourself to the Quran. Let Allah Subhanahu wa Ta'ala be your guide."

The student calls this man up. His name was Ahmed. He tells Ahmed, "Look, the Sheikh says don't turn yourself in. Allah Subhanahu wa Ta'ala wants you to rectify your ways. Turn back to Allah Subhanahu wa Ta'ala, and that is when that pain and suffering will be taken away."

That is what Ahmed decides to do. A couple of days go by. He starts reading the Quran. He starts praying in the masjid, and he says that he never missed a single Salah in the masjid since that event took place.

Now, the student disappears from the life of Ahmed. There was no contact between them. Then one day, he notices that he has a missed call from Ahmed. He says, "Later on, I'll give him a call." Another couple of days go by, and Ahmed's house is calling. Now his home number is showing up on the Sheikh's phone five, six times.

The student calls the house back and says, "As-Salamu Alaikum, how are you guys doing? What's going on?" And they say, "We need to speak to you. Everyone needs your help." And he says, "Definitely, I'll come over and see you tonight after Isha."

He prays Isha, heads over to the house, and sees that something just isn't right. He goes to the father and says, "As-Salamu Alaikum." He says, "Wa Alaikum As-Salam."

He says, "I don't even know what to say to you, but I want to thank you from the bottom of my heart because I know if it hadn't been for you, this wouldn't have happened." And the student is thinking, "What did I do?"

So he says, "You know what happened? What are you talking about?" And he says, "Let me show you." He says, "Ahmed went and prayed Salat al-Isha tonight, and he came back. He came to pray Sunnahs, and he was in his room for a really, really long time. We wanted to seek him out. We didn't know what had happened to him. But I want to show you."

He took the student to Ahmed's room, and there Ahmed was in sujood. Allah Subhanahu wa Ta'ala took his life away at that time. And that is how he passed away. This is the story of an individual who was not righteous. This man committed zina, one of the biggest sins in Islam, and this is how Allah Subhanahu wa Ta'ala took his life away. InshaAllah, when he's resurrected, that's the deed he's going to be resurrected on: making sujood to Allah Subhanahu wa Ta'ala.

Forsaking the Quran

A woman says that I was sitting in the area designated for women in the Haram of Makkah when a woman tapped me on the shoulder and started speaking in a foreign accent: "O pilgrim! O pilgrim!" When I turned towards her, I saw that she was a woman of middle age. I strongly suspect that she was of Turkish origin. She greeted me. Immediately, feelings of affection for her arose in my heart. SubhanAllah! These souls are also among the armies of Allah. Hearts have a way to each other. She wanted to say something to me and was gathering words to express her inner thoughts. She pointed to the Quran in my hand and then, in broken Arabic, asked: "Do you read the Quran?" I said: "Yes." As soon as she heard this, the woman's face turned red with joy and her eyes filled with tears. This sight made me anxious. The woman started crying. I asked her:

What's wrong with you?

She said, with shy eyes and a choked voice:

I cannot read the Quran.

I asked, why?

She replied that she was uneducated. As soon as this was on her lips, she burst into tears.

I kept patting her shoulder and comforting her. I said:

You are in the house of Allah, the Kaaba. Pray to Him to teach you the Quran and help you in learning its recitation and memorization. The woman wiped her tears.

I can never forget that scene for the rest of my life. The woman raised both her hands and began praying to Allah:

"O Allah! Open my chest so that I can read the Quran. O Allah! Open the doors of my heart so that I can read Your book."

Then she turned to me and said: I will die, but I will not be able to learn the Quran.

I told her:

That's not true. Insha'Allah, you will soon read the entire Quran and then complete it several times in your life.

I asked her:

Can you read Surah Al-Fatiha?

She happily said:

Yes! And then she began reading with great recitation:

"Praise be to Allah, the Lord of all the worlds. The Most Compassionate, the Most Merciful."

Until she had recited the entire Surah Al-Fatiha. Then she started reading the last Surahs of the Quran that she had memorized. I was amazed at her knowledge of Arabic and pronunciation, which was quite correct. She was telling me about her life and what she was doing to learn the Quran.

Suddenly, the color of her face changed and she said:

If I die and have not read the Quran, I will go to Hell. I swear by Allah! I have heard a cassette that says reading the Quran is obligatory. It is the word of Allah. The word of the Mighty Lord. As she was discussing the majesty of Allah and mentioning the rights of the Quran, she was making a great effort to hold back her tears, which were eager to spill from her eyes... I could not control myself and started crying uncontrollably.

I saw that a foreign woman, from a seemingly irreligious country, was afraid that she would meet her Lord in a state where she had not read His holy book. Her greatest wish in life was simply to read the entire Quran. She cried, was distressed, and became upset. All this was solely because she could not read the Quran!

What is our condition? We have abandoned the Quran. We read it, but have forgotten it. What is our state? While for us, memorizing the Quran, reciting it, and learning to understand it are very easy paths!

By Allah, tell me, what makes our hearts burn?

What is it that causes us to shed tears?

And what brings us sorrow and distress?

They were honored in their time by embracing Islam,

And you have become debased by forsaking the Quran.

We pray to Allah Almighty to make these incidents and stories beneficial and rewarding for people. Here we clarify that some of these events have been selected from certain websites on the internet. However, we could not find the names of the writers. Nevertheless, they are also equally deserving of reward, Insha'Allah.

In the end, I pray to Allah, the Generous and the Great, to unite us under His light in this world and the Hereafter. Allahumma Ameen.

Bibliography:

1. fī baṭni al-ḥūt .. Dr. Muḥammad bin 'Abd al-Raḥmān al-'Arīfī

2. I want to repent but... Sheikh Muhammed Salih Al-Munajjid